Vacation Houses

Aurora Cuito

HDi
HARPER
DESIGN
international

An Imprint of HarperCollins*Publishers*

Author: **Paco Asensio**

Editor: **Aurora Cuito**

Original text:
Aurora Cuito
Büchel House, Rosebery House, Into House, Rozelle-Ragan House, House in Vermont, Cabin at Masía Masnou, Burkhardt House, House in High Bridge, House for a Musician

Alejandro Bahamón
Kessler House, Two-Family Duplex, Furniture House, Bach House, Barry's Bay Cottage, Arrowleaf House, Wilson House, Loken Residence, House in Moledo, Parker-Huber House, Heidi House, Summer House

Belén García
YG House, Ravenwood House

Translation: **Michael Bunn**

Proofreading: **Julie King**

Design: **Mireia Casanovas Soley**

Layout: **Jaume Martínez, Diego González**

Editorial project

LOFT Publications
Via Laietana, 32 4º Of. 92
08003 Barcelona. Spain
Tel.: +34 932 688 088
Fax: +34 932 687 073
e-mail: loft@loftpublications.com
www.loftpublications.com

Printed by: Anman Gràfiques del Vallès, Sabadell. Spain
www.anman.com

DL: B-26743-04

First printing, 2004

INTRODUCTION

This book contains a selection of vacation houses that have been built in mountainous regions. These houses have used the environment as an inspiration to its architecture. While vacationing, one wants to see tranquility when looking out the window rather than the hustle and bustle of every day life. Yet this tranquility has its own price to pay: the climate of the environment that it lies within. Mother nature does not play favorites to anyone or anyplace. Vacationing in a mountainous environment can be subject to drastic climatic conditions that may have serious consequences on the lifestyle of the inhabitants. As a result, all of the projects featured here incorporate elements that serve to combat the extremes of the different climates, while still allowing the owners to enjoy the beautiful landscape around them.

Climate is, undoubtedly, one of the main factors to consider when planning construction in the mountains. The entire process, from the design stage to the choice of materials, depends on the specific atmospheric conditions of a particular location. Everything has to be organized around sunlight, humidity, temperature variations, and wind speed and direction.

One of the recurring architectural priorities is to maximize the amount of sunshine entering the constructions. During the winter and in areas far away from the equator, sunshine is scarce. The designers utilize many architectural strategies in order to take as much advantage of the warm light as they can.

High relative humidity is another factor that creates problems for the residents. The moisture in the air means that summers are muggy and sticky, while cold air seems to penetrate even more in the winter. Humidity can be dangerous to houses situated in such climates, since it adds to the constructional wear and tear. Condensation on walls and floors causes damp stains, especially in the areas of the house that are in contact with the land. Poor ventilation of interior spaces can also cause problems, such as the rusting of pipes and other metal features.

Finally, snow is one of the most important factors that determines the final shape of the project and the choice of materials. Almost all the roofs of the houses contained in this book have been equipped with some mechanism or special design that prevents the snow from accumulating, thereby avoiding the problems of added weight on the structure and an increase in humidity.

Apart from the climate, the topographical location and the orientation of the structure also need to be taken into account when planning a mountain house. The difficulties that must be overcome include a site that contains a pronounced slope, vegetation and the absence of a main water connection.

Tourism and speculation have brought about the destruction of some wonderful landscapes. But in recent years, the awakening of our ecological awareness has resulted in the creation of natural parks and the implementation of national and international regulations to prevent further damage to the environment. The house designs included in this book have been strongly influenced by this philosophy, and a common feature that stands out in all of them is the inherent respect they show toward the land on which they have been built and the vacationers who enjoy their homes in this tranquil and safe environment.

—Paco Asensio

Jim Brandenburg discovered this site in Northwoods, Minnesota, in 1979 while on a trip to photograph a waterfall in Superior National Forest for *National Geographic* magazine. The lot, near the waterfall and bordering the Boundary Waters Canoe Area, was where Jim would photograph the wolves that appeared in his highly successful book *Brother Wolf*, published in 1993. In 1981, Jim and his wife, Judy, who were at that time living in Minneapolis, had a vacation home built out of cedar logs, right in the middle of the forest. The house was made up of four small structures—a main cabin, guest house, sauna, and bathroom—all arranged like steps on the side of the hill. Time passed, and the Brandenburgs decided to enlarge the cabin so they could live in it for longer periods of time. With this in mind, they contacted architect David Salmela. Brandenburg envisioned an elongated house, reminiscent of a Viking longhouse. Salmela followed his instructions and added several gable-roofed structures arranged around an external patio, all in keeping with the existing buildings stylistically. The original cabin has a kitchen on the lower level with a double room upstairs. The main building, approximately 4,575 square feet, is angled at 45 degrees to the southwest with respect to the original cabin, to which it connects through the

DAVID SALMELA

☐ RAVENWOOD HOUSE

NORTHWOODS, MINNESOTA, USA. 1998   PHOTOGRAPHY: PETER KERZE

first story space containing the dining room and gallery. This building has three clearly differentiated sections: one of double height with a storeroom and bathroom, another two-story section with a living room below and guest room above, and a third, which has three levels—the main study, a computer area, and a loft at the top. At the other side of the driveway, a second structure has a study on the first floor and a storeroom above. The

contiguous semicircular space, which is topped by a grassy roof and serves as the garage, is ideal for conferences and seminars. Cedar planks are mounted vertically onto the exterior walls of the new buildings. Most of the interior finishing employs the same wood, although maple is used for the horizontal features and the flooring is slate. All the new structures have been stained black, the same shade used to paint the cedar logs of the pre-existing buildings.

This results in a camouflaged appearance, but also brings us back to the Vikings, for this is the same blackish hue that pine acquires with age when used for damp areas in houses and for boats.

☐ Ravenwood was awarded a national prize in 1997 by the American Institute of Architects (AIA) as well as an award from the AIA in Minnesota. This has given David Salmela some well-deserved recognition.

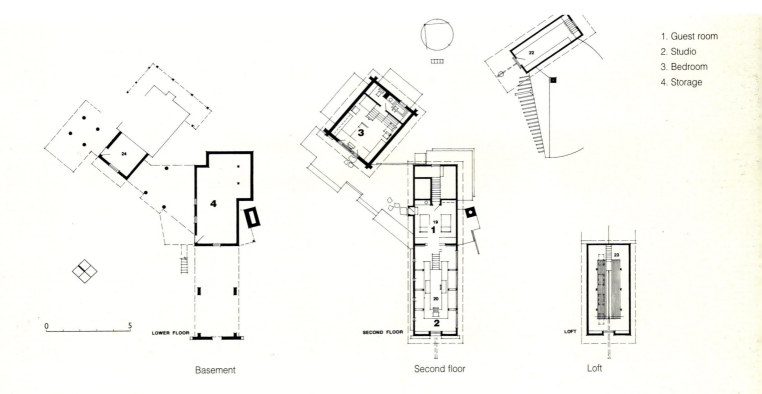

1. Guest room
2. Studio
3. Bedroom
4. Storage

Basement   Second floor   Loft

☐ Salmela's work springs directly from his strong commitment to the architectural interpretation of his clients' wishes and tastes. The results can seem almost magical.

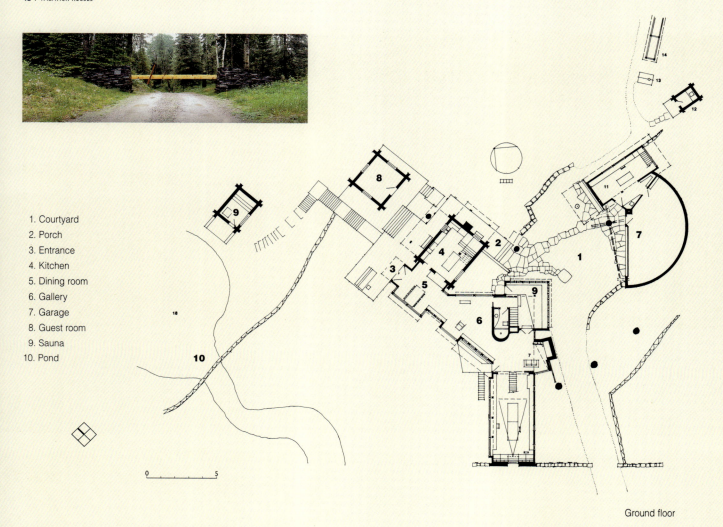

1. Courtyard
2. Porch
3. Entrance
4. Kitchen
5. Dining room
6. Gallery
7. Garage
8. Guest room
9. Sauna
10. Pond

0 _____ 5

Ground floor

□ Above: view of the room with the doors open. The little loft up the stairs can be
seen. Right: the doors, made of wood and translucent panels, are closed, and
there is no visual connection between either space.

This project, by Jyrki Tasa in Espoo, Finland, is an object lesson in combining poetic exercise with rational execution. The most advanced, precise techniques are employed to create a symbiosis in a contemporary, sensual, and highly imaginative structure. The site is located on a high, west-facing hill overlooking the sea. The house seems small atop the rock, which gives the impression that it is desperately holding onto the outcrop. The building has protection, however, in the form of a white curving wall. The construction profile fans out to enclose a warm and welcoming home on one side, while on the other, it seals off the house from the cold weather coming down from the north. The building is clearly organized into different sections, but despite the methodical, practical distribution of the space, the house is free from any inert rigidity. This is partly due to the use of two very different elements: powerful, evocative steel and beautiful, obliging wood. The combination creates warm, welcoming finishes. Following the winding highway, the visitor gets an occasional glimpse of the undulating eaves and the tall columns on the west facade, features that hint at the house's dual nature. The road leads to the rear of the house, which is delineated by the white, protective wall. The main entrance is a glass fissure in the facade, which is accessed by a metal bridge that crosses over the swimming pool. Once you cross this bridge, you leave behind the neighboring buildings and enter a space designed for the appreciation of nature, whether inside or in its wilder form, as seen from the terraces and balconies. The entrance hall acts as a connecting point, both visually and functionally, for all the areas within the house, whose excep-

JYRKI TASA

☐ INTO HOUSE

ESPOO, FINLAND. 1998   PHOTOGRAPHY: JUSSI TIANEN & JYRKI TASA

tional height and expansive windows offer magnificent views. The house can be perceived and understood in its entirety from this entrance hall, which links the living spaces with the more private rooms. Vertical features define this central section: the steel and wood stairway, which exudes structural and sculptural virtuosity, and the tower that houses the chimneys. This tower pierces the entire structure, accentuating and dramatizing the vertical environment: the mountain and its rocky landscape. The house was designed for a bachelor, and the layout emphasizes the daytime areas, ideal places for informal get-togethers. In comparison, the bedrooms and bathroom are relatively small. The terraces and balconies play important roles in the arrangement of the house. All have specific functions besides being marvelous vantage points. By silhouetting the house, Tasa creates an effect of double transparency, thereby drawing attention to different aspects of the exterior construction. The intention of this well-known Finnish architect was to balance the major architectural features and the specific details of the construction. Stability is achieved by revealing the materials in their purest form and by painstakingly incorporating features such as sliding doors, woodwork, handles, and handrails. This constructional coherence is highlighted by the specially designed lighting, featuring attractive wall lamps. The effect is consolidated through other elements, such as the extractor fan, the glass shelving in the kitchen, the dining room furniture, the living room lamps, and the external lighting.

☐ Into House rises out of a solid rock outcrop. Its appearance is reminiscent of traditional nomadic constructions, with the metal roof resting on cylindrical metal sections, as if it were a sheet of protective material stretched out over a series of poles.

1. Garage
2. Utility room
3. Storeroom
4. Guest bedroom
5. Swimming pool
6. Sauna
7. Laundry
8. Entrance
9. Bedrooms
10. Living room
11. Dining room
12. Kitchen

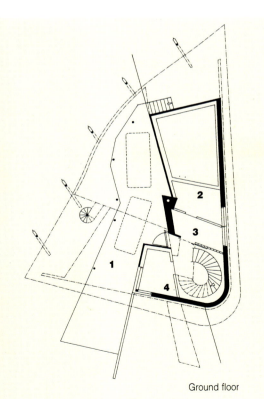

Ground floor

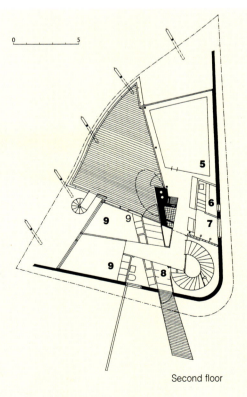

Second floor

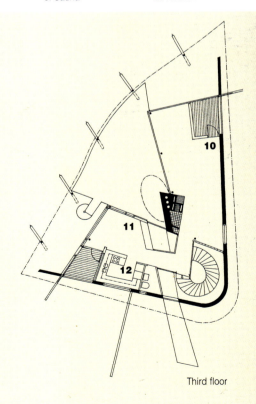

Third floor

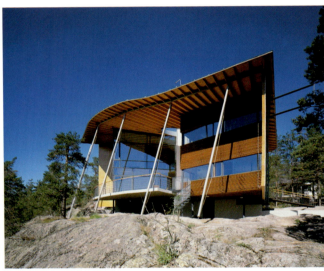

☐ The axonometric perspective clearly shows the structural organization of the house: A framework of metal pillars and other vertical features support an arrangement of beams. The back wall affords horizontal rigidity to the structure. The opaque and impermeable north-facing enclosure was designed to isolate the structure from the neighboring properties and the cold winds. A bridge over the pool leads up to the entrance, which is the only opening in the wall.

☐ The back wall provides privacy and the necessary horizontal structural rigidity. The external spaces have specific functions, and all afford magnificent forest views. In addition, the serpentine lines of the second floor make various construction details visible.

☐ Wood predominates in the interior. The flooring is cherrywood and the vertical partitions are made of pine. This combination results in practical and functional spaces that are also comfortable and attractive. The natural light from the skylights and the large windows bring out the different textures of the wood.

☐ The stairway, composed of a folded sheet of pinewood supported by a light structure of steel tubing and metal cables, is made possible by the application of exacting engineering skills.

Japan has produced an abundance of architects during the twentieth century, many of who have created extremely interesting works. Born between 1925 and 1938, Arata Isozaki, Kisho Kurokawa, Fumihiko Maki and Kazuo Shinohara (also known as "the Four Greats") paved the way for the post-war "Baby Boom" generation of excellent architects (including Tadao Ando, Itsuko Hasegawa, Katsuhiro Ishii, Toyo Ito, Kiko Mozuna, Kijo Rokkaku, Shin Takamatsu, Shoei Yoh, and Riken Yamamoto).

Hitoshi Abe, head of Atelier Hitoshi Abe, belongs to an even later generation of architects. A contemporary of Shigeru Ban and Kazuyo Sejima, he was born in 1962. He worked for the Himmelblau Cooperative for four years until he founded Atelier Hitoshi Abe with Yosikatu Matuno and Hideyuki Mori.

In the early 1990s, Atelier accepted numerous relatively large commissions, including the Miyagi stadium, the water tower at Miyagi, the Shirasagi and Natori bridges, and the temporary museum known as "XX-Box." In the late 1990s, however, the company began to take on more intimate projects, such as the two houses "M-House" and "Gravel-2," and the "Neige lune fleur" restaurant. It was during this period that the plans were drafted for YG House, located in Katta-gun, Japan.

The structure, designed as a strip 750 feet in length, winds back onto itself in three dimensions, leaving a large central space. Six different components, the functional areas needed to make the house livable, have been grafted onto the length of this strip. Specifically, these components are a fireplace/closet, a kitchen, a toilet/ laundry, a bath, a shoe closet, and a

ATELIER HITOSHI ABE

☐ YG HOUSE

KATTA-GUN, JAPAN. 1997   PHOTOGRAPHY: SYUNICHI ATSUMI

storeroom.

The two-story, enclosed central space, an extraordinary space in the context of the dwelling, is unquestionably the nucleus of the house. While the six volumes are all enclosed—opening only when functionally necessary—the central space is designed to communicate directly with the exterior, either through the views or the natural light, thereby establishing different relationships with the external surroundings.

The building appears very narrow in relation to its site. To the north, the entrance area follows the contour lines, while the vol-ume, having touched the dwelling tangentially, leaves the ground toward the southern end. The centripetal movement of the interior envelops the entire height of the central space as the viewer ascends the stairways, passing by the chimney flue and along the corridor, moving farther and farther from ground level.

This upward-moving spiral path is accented by two crucial design decisions. First, the contrast between light (the white stairway wall and the fireplace) and dark (the cedar wood used for the floors and walls), which effectively delineates the route, and second, the suggestive arrangement of sloping roof sections, which helps to show, from the outside, what is going on inside.

This project is an ambitious yet viable effort to transform an abstract vision into a physical structure within a certain context.

☐ YG House was designed as a weekend residence for guests of the company that commissioned the project. It stands on a 0.348 acre lot at the highest point of a south-facing piece of land. The two-story, 1,324 square foot house seems to be completely surrounded by trees.

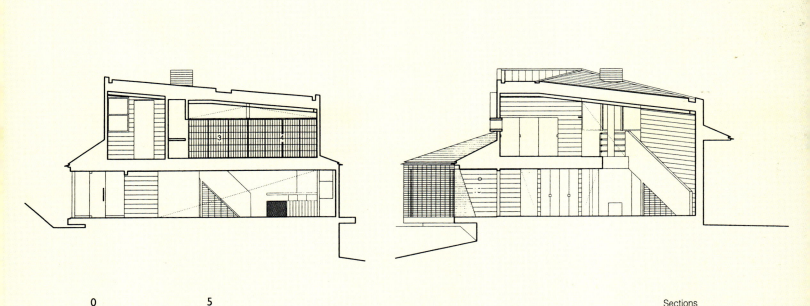

0 _____ 5

Sections

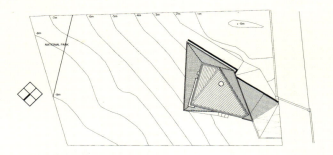

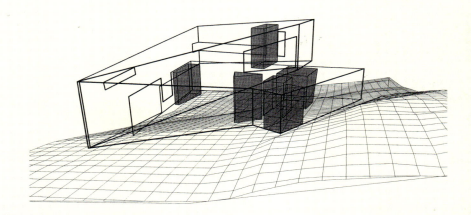

☐ Atelier Hitoshi Abe used computer simulations to visualize the relationship of the land to the house. The virtual profiles they created enabled them to study, in advance, the house's effect on the landscape and the natural environment.

☐ Although the lines of the house are strictly geometric, the effect is softened by the materials, mostly wood, which harmonize with the forest landscape. The terraces and the other outdoor areas can be used as common spaces, since they are shaded from the sun by a system of wooden strips. This makes the space available for year-round activities, since the weather here is never particularly harsh.

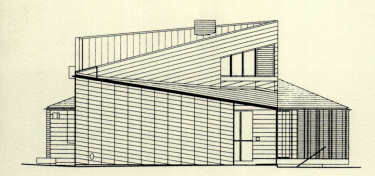

North elevation

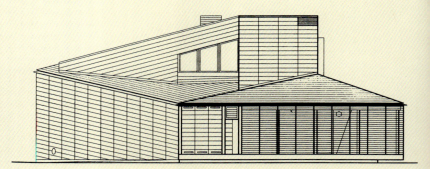

West elevation

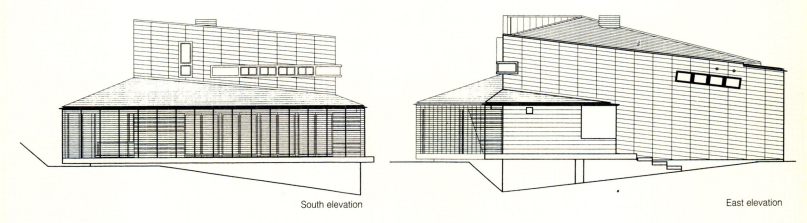

South elevation

East elevation

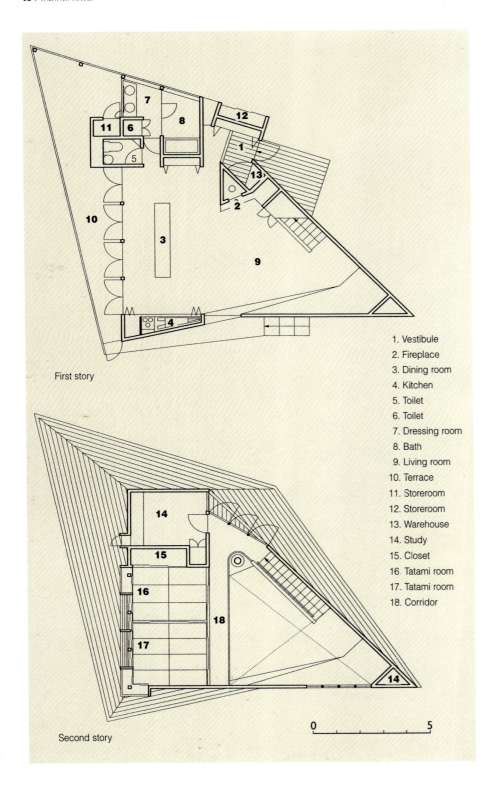

First story

Second story

0   5

1. Vestibule
2. Fireplace
3. Dining room
4. Kitchen
5. Toilet
6. Toilet
7. Dressing room
8. Bath
9. Living room
10. Terrace
11. Storeroom
12. Storeroom
13. Warehouse
14. Study
15. Closet
16. Tatami room
17. Tatami room
18. Corridor

□ The sparse furnishings, which make this perfectly functional as a weekend home, are counterbalanced by the warm tones of the wood, an element that is used both inside and out.

The design of this weekend home in Ontario, Canada, is largely an extended formal study of the different ways to use one particular material: wood. The manner in which this material has been incorporated into both the spatial distribution and the interior space is inspired by careful observation of the basic characteristics of the landscape. The design concept presented here by these two New York– based Iranian architects involves the abstraction of these natural features and their subsequent synthesis into the structural composition, down to the most subtle details. The rural site in Ontario, Canada, is defined by two main natural features: an abundance of deciduous trees, including tall birches, and gently sloping land, which leads to the still waters of Lake Kamaniskeg. It is a peaceful setting, ideal for meditation; the line where the lake meets the shore contrasts with the tree line by the water's edge. The objective of the project was to expand an A-frame prefabricated cabin that the family, now six people, had outgrown. The client's fondness for the old cabin led to its incorporation into the new design as a section for the children and guests. The existing structure was used as a point of departure, and it subsequently became an important element of the new construction.

The false shutters were removed, the pink paint stripped from the walls, and the asphalt roof tiles replaced by galvanized steel panels, which were more in keeping

HARIRI & HARIRI

☐ # BARRY'S BAY COTTAGE

ONTARIO, CANADA. 1994   PHOTOGRAPHY: JOHN M. HALL

with the language of the new construction. However, only minimal changes were made in the interior: The living room was replaced by a large kitchen, and a dining room was incorporated into the lower story. The new cabin is a wooden structure, nearly 100 feet long, which extends along the western boundary of the property, less than 7 feet from the original structure. It contains the main bedroom, a library, a reading room, a large living room, and a boathouse. The elongated shape of the structure allowed the old trees to be left in place and preserved the open space in front of the old cabin. This area creates a curious dynamic tension between the old and new buildings, which is common with rural constructions. The old and new structures are connected by a large wooden deck, which is raised off the ground by concrete pillars and complemented by the surrounding elements. Initially, it is just a flat section compressed between the two buildings, which frame a narrow view of the lake. However, moving forward along the deck, the view opens up gradually until it suddenly widens out at a point above the level of the lake. At the far edge of the deck, a staircase descends approximately 10 feet to the ground. Beside the staircase, at ground level, there is a small outdoor shower room, which also has a framed view of the lake and can be used as a private space for reflection and relaxation to escape the stresses of everyday life.

☐ The main material used in this house is red cedar, while white maple was used for the floors and galvanized metal panels were used for the roof.

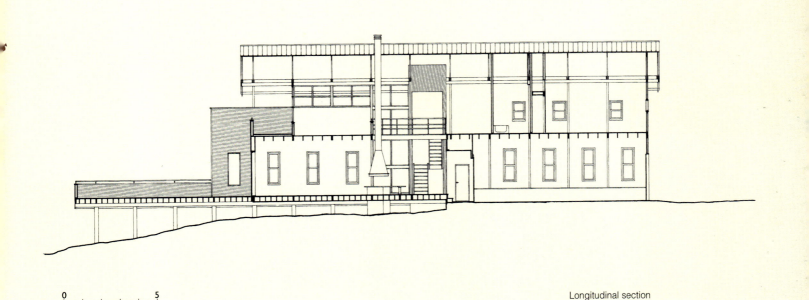

0   5

Longitudinal section

The groove windows are an important feature of the new section's exterior walls. Intended to frame the views, they were inspired by the horizontal patterns on the bark of the birch trees that surround the house. As a result, the house becomes a structure of posts and beams, with external walls resembling curtains. In the daytime, the windows frame different sections of the landscape behind the building and let the natural light into the interior. At night, they serve as lamps, visible from outside. In contrast, the west side emphasizes the verticality of the tall trees in the surrounding fields, synthesized through elements such as the corrugated iron staircase tower.

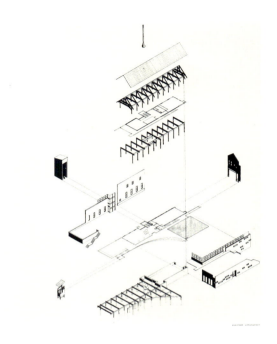

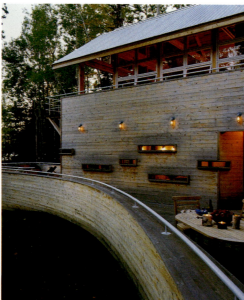

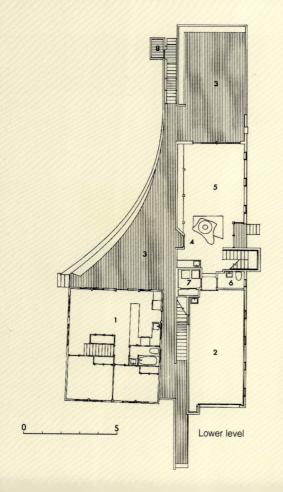

Lower level

0   5

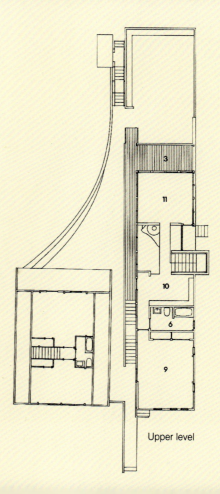

Upper level

The interior of the new house includes a large living room with a fireplace in the center under a suspended chimney. On the upper level, a bridge connects the reading room and library, open to the living room below, to the main bedroom at the north end. A deck on the upper story, adjacent to the reading room, creates a private space for contemplation and rest.

At first sight, this house in Moledo, Portugal, seems to emerge from one of the hills. A single-story construction in the form of an elongated rectangle, it rests on a hillside facing the sea.

In this project, the architect established a close relationship between object and landscape based on two complementary elements, the terraced site, which may have cost more than the actual house and the use of a very pure architectural language, common to the work of this architect and reminiscent of the mid-twentieth century rationalist approach to housing.

The modern design comes out in both the floor plan and the materials, as well as the way they are used. For example, glass and thin aluminum sections define the arrangement of corridors, and these materials frame the organic texture of the stone. This effectively draws attention from the stone to the metal and glass, and then back again to the stone. This is the key to the spatial logic of the project, which, according to de Moura, was borrowed directly from the traditional Portuguese house. There is a local tradition of terracing the uneven land for agriculture and construc-

tion. The house was built high on the hill, presenting a kind of optical illusion. Through a large opening in the stone wall, which complements the stone in the embankment and perfectly integrates the structure into the mountain landscape, you can see the house with its predominance of glass surfaces and horizontal reinforced concrete roof. The glass is interrupted by a door/sliding window module, but, continuing along this side of the structure, it makes for a light, transparent building that hides nothing from the natural surroundings. Chimneys and extractor

EDUARDO SOUTO DE MOURA

☐ HOUSE IN MOLEDO

MOLEDO, PORTUGAL. 1998   PHOTOGRAPHY: LUIS FERREIRA ALVÉS

ducts emerge from the roof—industrial-style minimalist features as sophisticated architecture. At the rear of the house, a patio has been incorporated, which is a simple way of separating the structure from the mountain and at the same time ensuring light and ventilation on both sides.

The interior of this family residence is organized linearly, with a corridor running along the back of the house toward the interior patio, while the living spaces face the ocean. The living room and dining room, which are arranged together in a single space beside the entrance, open out toward both sides, creating a kind of ball-and-socket effect. On one side is the kitchen, which extends into an external patio, while the other side contains the bedrooms and a small study. The partitions that divide the rooms keep the interior free of supporting columns, so the elements in the interior space, framed by a continuous glass surface on both sides, are minimized. The same stone used outside was brought into the house for the wall separating the living room and the kitchen, creating a marked division between the two areas. However, wooden panels were used for the other walls to demarcate the bedrooms and the corridor. In projects such as this, in which the structural elements are reduced to the very minimum in order to emphasize the different spatial values, enormous care must be taken in designing each detail. This house is an excellent example of the rigor with which de Moura introduces the different features and elements into a structure, manipulating each with the utmost care until everything harmonizes, to produce an arrangement that is both pure and restrained.

☐ Projects such as this one, which downplay the construction elements in order to emphasize other values of the space, require great attention to detail. This house highlights the rigor of architect Eduardo Souto de Moura, who controls every detail to achieve an austere effect.

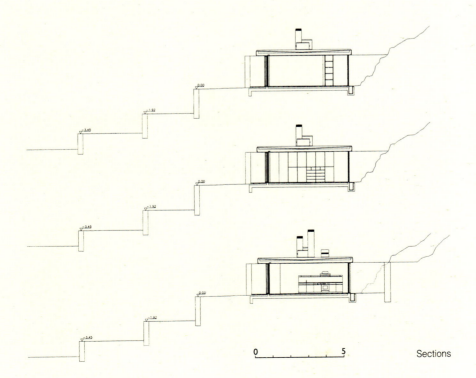

0   5   Sections

☐ The roof, the element that gives away the presence of the house, can be seen from the
top of the mountain. Ventilation ducts and chimneys are above the roof.

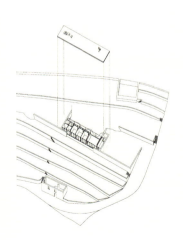 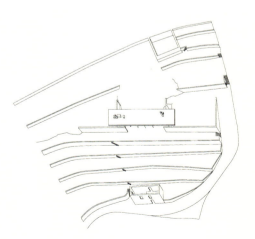

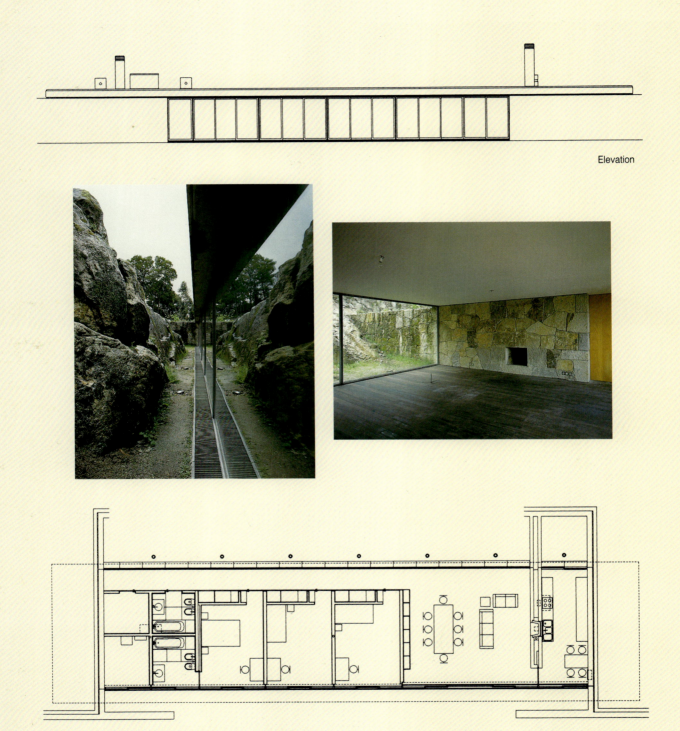

Elevation

Floor plan

In the case of Büchel House, architectural firm, Baumschlager and Eberle did not regard the commission simply as an opportunity to explore available artistic avenues. Rather, they saw it as a chance to create a building in harmony with society's needs—a product embracing civic values such as economy, practicality and comfort. And though this concept might result in architectural blandness, (houses that are simply restrained and discreetly contained), Baumschlager and Eberle design constructions that are openly original and aesthetically pleasing while maintaining a commitment to economy and ecological principles.

The Büchel residence, a mountain house occupying a strip of hillside speckled with fruit trees beneath Vaduz Castle in Liechtenstein, has a solitary air, but at the same time serves as a landscape enhancing protagonist within the topography. This relationship between the structure and the natura surroundings was achieved through intense discussion between the architects and clients. The architects' priority was to make the most out of the topographical features while preserving the surrounding orchards. Accordingly, they chose a compact, three-story structure instead of one extending horizontally, which would have taken up more space to the detriment of the natural surroundings. The inverted-step arrangement, incorporated into the southern facade which overlooks the valley, may appear to be simply the result of a trivial aesthetic decision, but in reality it provides a masterly touch which enables the building to gain space on each story, minimizing the demands on the available lot space. The project is focused on the functional requirements of each interior space, and

BAUMSCHLAGER & EBERLE
☐ # BÜCHEL HOUSE
VADUZ, LIECHTENSTEIN. 1996 PHOTOGRAPHY: EDUARD HUEBER

the exterior walls are given four different faces, according to the way in which the design is laid out horizontally. Three of the faces are concrete surfaces that have been finished with extreme care. The north side is totally closed to the weak light and low temperatures and is broken only by two openings, the garage door and a high narrow window that echoes the vertical lines of the structure. The west face has been more freely designed and its openings are less restricted. The introspection suggested by these faces changes completely when one reaches the south wall. On this side, large windows open up the house to the magnificent view of the valley. The woodworking is purposely light and discreet so as to minimally interfere with the line of sight. Protection from the sun is provided by folding wooden blinds that can be adjusted to control the amount of light entering the house. The interior lighting is another aspect to which the designers have paid particular attention: The darkest parts of the house are illuminated through specific construction details, such as a skylight above the stairway and the fanlight above the entrance hall on the upper floor. As a result, the interior benefits from both additional light and easy access to the exterior vistas. The terrace, located to the west of the first story, also plays an important role. Seemingly suspended in the air, it effectively extends outward the dining room and creates an exterior living space that can be utilized simply by opening a sliding door.

□ The house is located on what could be called a dual landscape. On one side, the land is suddenly truncated by a rocky cliff, while on the other lies a fruit tree–filled valley that stretches up to Vaduz Castle.

Eastern elevation

Transversal elevation

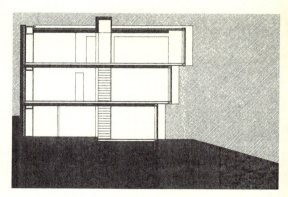

Longitudinal elevation

☐ The project can be considered an arrangement for a specific location. The imposing rock face, left over from an abandoned quarry, serves as a backdrop to the house, creating textural continuity with the concrete surface of the walls.

Baumschlager and Eberle's success results directly from their commitment to an architectural approach that combines two highly desirable elements: cost-effectiveness and adherence to sound ecological principles. It should come as no surprise that their designs have been praised by builders, public officials, and private clients alike. These two Austrian architects have adopted a simple, rational, and elegant architectural style which is attuned to current tastes. They do not create unusual structures; rather, they specialize in a type of architecture that blends craftsmanship with industrial production while maintaining a healthy balance between cost and output. The results are houses which have unquestionable architectural value, built within modest budgets. When it comes to experimentation with construction techniques, detached houses are the most sought-after projects for any architect.

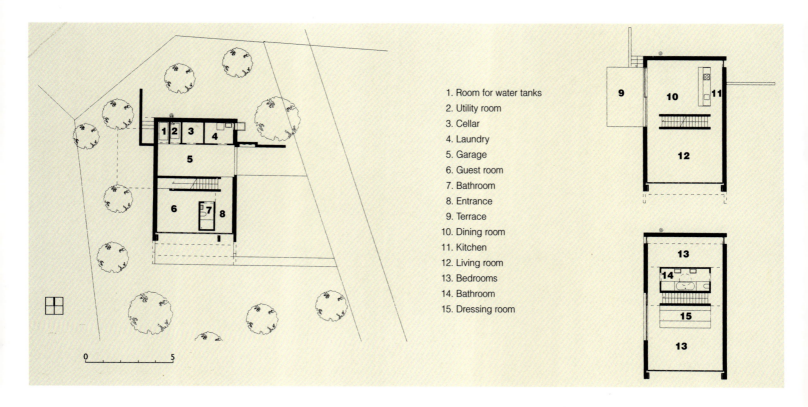

1. Room for water tanks
2. Utility room
3. Cellar
4. Laundry
5. Garage
6. Guest room
7. Bathroom
8. Entrance
9. Terrace
10. Dining room
11. Kitchen
12. Living room
13. Bedrooms
14. Bathroom
15. Dressing room

☐ Each detail results from a painstaking design process. A good example is provided by the glass expanses set into the walls, with wooden blinds that slide or fold open and shut.

This project is not exactly a house; it is a small refuge in the northern mountains of Washington State. The client, who is extremely fond of the region's landscape, wanted a structure where he could stay for short periods and that would afford views of the spectacular area. The concept was to construct a small, modest building that would respect the natural environment while providing all the comforts of home.

The starting point for the design was the question of how to situate the structure on the site. The building is raised off the ground by ten reinforced concrete pillars. These maintain the continuity of the ground as much as possible while solving the problem of how to give the structure a level floor, since the lot in question is on the slope of a hill. The house that stands on this base slab is essentially a box with a gable roof, both made of wood. The base has two openings: One on the southern side provides access to the interior while a larger one on the northern side opens onto a terrace with a panoramic view. A stairway descends from the terrace to the ground, where a path leads straight into the forest. The exterior surface has been carefully finished with thin wood strips, incorporated into the structure to create a delicate visual texture. This covering almost disappears on the north side, where wood is replaced by glass. Large windows create direct communication among the interior space, the terrace, and the forest. The continuation of the wooden structure, in the form of a supporting framework for the roof, is an intentional device that helps blur the borders between the interior and the exte-

JAMES CUTLER
□ ARROWLEAF HOUSE
METHOW VALLEY, WASHINGTON USA. 1998   PHOTOGRAPHY: ART GRICE

rior in this area of the house.

The interior is a simple layout on two levels. Entering the lower section through the door and passing through the small hall, we find the kitchen, dining room, and living room, all laid out in a single space. The second level contains the bathroom and the two bedrooms, one of which is enclosed while the other opens out directly onto the living room. The bath and toilet, the stairway, and part of the furniture take up the lateral walls, freeing the interior space and focusing attention on the exit to the terrace. In a beautiful blend of light and dark tones, wood is the predominant material inside, where it has been used for the floor, doors, windows, hand rails and furniture.

The architect designed the details to bring out the structural features and draw attention to the materials from which the house was built. Each piece (for example, the wall panels) is intended to highlight the way the house was built and bring out the wood's natural color. Thus, the architect successfully uses this project to pay hom-age to the materials used, allowing them to speak for themselves and creating a beautiful dwelling that is closely linked to, yet protected from, the natural world. It is a space that avoids falling into the trap of formal excess. Instead, it provides warm, elementary lines that perfectly serve the purpose for which they were designed: a refuge.

☐ The way in which the house is supported by concrete pillars and suspended above the ground establishes a close link between the buildings and the natural surroundings. Each one enhances the other.

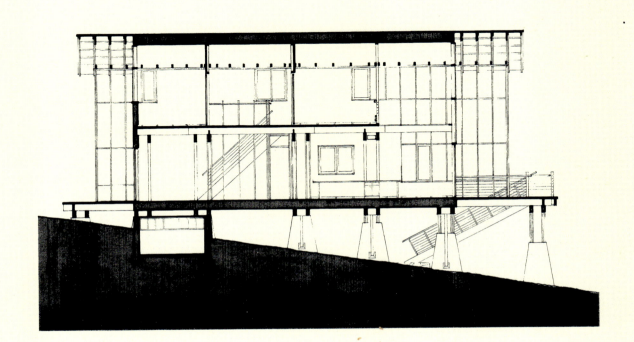

In this project, the architect's intention was to respect every material used in the construction so that each would speack for itself and enrich the experience of its tenants. The result is a simple, warm space in which to encounter a sense of refuge.

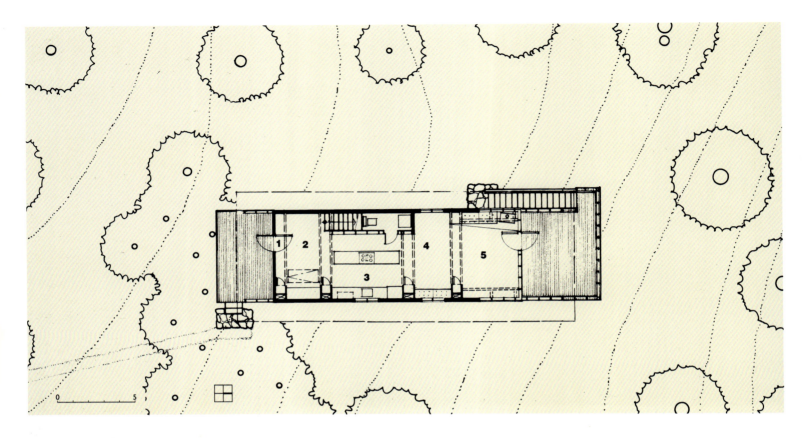

☐ While the space is continuous, each corner manages to preserve its own character through the use of materials, the positioning of the furniture, and the perception from the upper and lower floors. Each architectural piece and detail is treated so that one can appreciate its natural color, origin, and the way it was constructed. Even the individual panels that make up the walls are visible.

1. Hallway
2. Foyer
3. Kitchen
4. Living room
5. Terrace

In this project, both the expressiveness of the different forms and materials and the way in which the house relates to the mountain follow specific design criteria, which results in a solid, sustainable structure with a flexible distribution plan. The general concept emerges from five fundamental, closely interconnected principles, which this American architect employs consistently: maximization of available energy resources, the roof as protective skin, the central area of the house as the very heart of the project, use of pure geometric forms, and respect for the envi-ronmental context.

The goal of maximizing energy resources springs from the architect's desire to unite the building and its natural environment. This is achieved by ensuring that as much natural light as possible enters the house, located on the south side of a hill in the middle of a North Carolina forest, with breathtaking views of the surrounding area near Charlotte. The warm light that the southern side receives persuaded the architect to arrange the living and sleeping areas along this part of the house. This means that in winter, the light enters and warms the areas in which the inhabitants spend most of their time. The structure also has a solar energy unit; photovoltaic cells along the north wall form an external gallery and function as a transition between the building and the mountain.

The spatial distribution inside the house is defined by the arrangement of gable roofs, which symbolize home and provide a feeling of security, "the protective skin." This type of roof also allows the architect to subtly manipulate the buildings' various symmetries in order to create harmony between the different spaces (for example

ALFREDO DE VIDO

☐ KESSLER HOUSE

CHARLOTTE, NORTH CAROLINA, USA. 1996   PHOTOGRAPHY: ALFREDO DE VIDO

the porch off the front door of the house has a small gable-roofed structure that is, in effect, a tiny version of the house itself). The bedrooms are defined by similar small roofing sections laid out in steps, thus establishing a relationship with the exterior.

At the heart of the project is the highest and most dynamic space: a space made up of the living room, the dining room, and the kitchen that are combined into a single living area which connects itself to all the other parts of the house. An area in which the concept of home is most concentrated, it serves as the east-west axis of the building. The fireplace, with its rustic ceramic finish, functions independently within the room, while it articulates the access areas, corridors, and living space. Here, the spatial elements, such as the sloping roof sections, skylights, fireplace, kitchen table, and extractor hood, almost become sculpted objects that are accentuated by the natural light.

The linear design of the home uses geometric forms to arrange the spatial distribution of each room. The layout of the home starts with an elongated rectangle that contains the living room and the two bedrooms. Attached to this space is a shorter rectangle containing the kitchen and dining room.

The fifth compositional principle of the project, respect for the environmental context, is virtually a corollary of the first four.

☐ The formal repertoire of the house consists of squares, triangles, and rectangles (seen on the floor plan). This results in a simple, easily understood building. For De Vido, geometry is the source of rational organization as well as the best way to view the natural world.

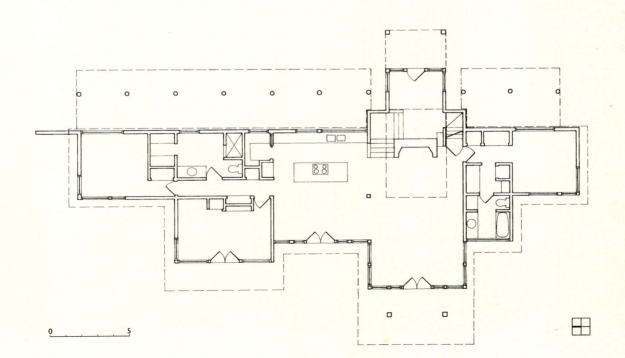

0 _____ 5

☐ The house incorporates architectural elements and materials typical of the region, such as wood and iron. The owners, who are skilled craftsmen, designed many of the house's features, such as the metal grills, the extractor hood, and the fire irons.

The lot on which this house was built is near the road leading into the town of High Bridge, New Jersey. In the eighteenth century, it was the site of an iron mine that produced raw material for the cannon balls manufactured at a nearby factory. The parcel is densely wooded, mostly with oaks and maples, and has a pronounced slope. The elevation change from one end of the lot to the other is nearly 120 feet. The area's extensive greenery is marred only by a few scars from an attempt to reopen the mines in the 1980s. A creek, very popular among local residents for hiking and fishing, flows down from the neighboring hills and runs through the site near the structure.

The building is home to an executive during the workweek, who spends weekends in the city. The focus of the project was to create a house that was compact, adaptable and easily accessible. The client required three bedrooms, although two were to be somewhat flexible with regard to size and use, with two and a half baths, as well as a library, an office, and a two-car garage. He envisioned the dining room, living room, and kitchen as an extension of the landscape that somehow incorporated itself into the rest of the structure.

The house follows the contours of the land to the extent that the architecture embodies the existing topography. Parts of the mine works, open spaces waiting to be reclaimed by the ever-encroaching forest, are still visible from inside the house. The structural agenda of the site was a major

KRAMER E. WOODARD ARCHITECTS
☐ HOUSE IN HIGH BRIDGE
HIGH BRIDGE, NEW JERSEY, USA. 1998   PHOTOGRAPHY: KEVIN CHU AND CATHERINE TIGHE BOGERT

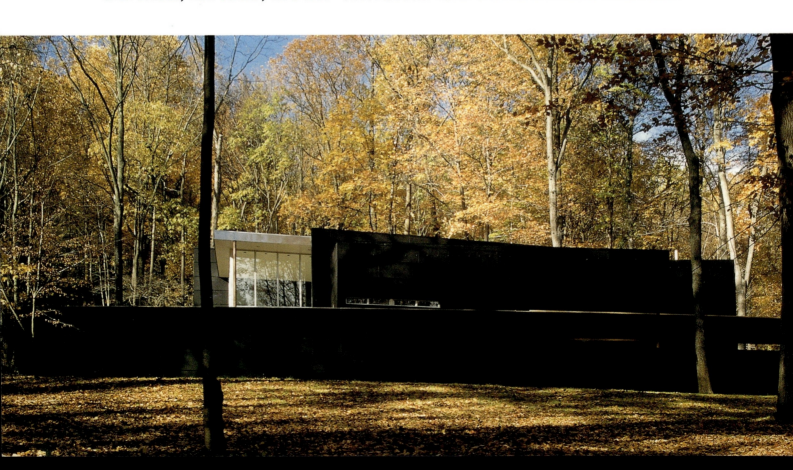

factor in plan development, and the original mines are echoed by the formal lines of the new construction, an arrangement of horizontal strips parallel to the gradient. A system of thick and thin walls creates an alternating series of rooms and open areas, the latter resembling lenses focused on the structural layout. The building is the mise-en-scène for an exploration of the plasticity of architectural space through the passage of time.

The house was built with traditional construction techniques and common materials. Conceptually, the project was intended to explore the idea of interior space as an extension of the landscape, or vice versa, rather than to experiment with the use of new materials and methods for adapting the structure to the land.

The house has concrete foundations and walls that combine cement fiber sheets, stone, and wood. A variety of finishes—ceramic tile, varnished wood, and polished stone—were used inside. The choice of materials gives the house a geode like appearance: The regularity of the exterior gives away little of the beautiful, crystalline interior. The lighting, drains, and heating installations were also made with conventional materials and techniques.

☐ The house has the appearance of a geological feature, the result, one might think, of mining excavations that took place on the site at the end of the eighteenth century. The walls emerge from the land, perpendicular to the slope.

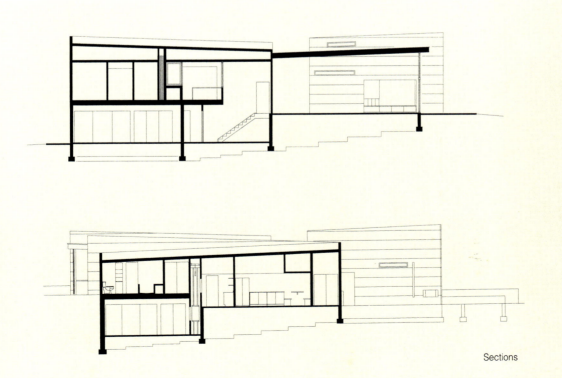

Sections

 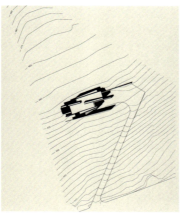 

☐ The garage takes up the lower level of the structure, while the living spaces are on the upper level, interwoven within the exterior walls of the house. These walls are positioned so that they seem to be separated by spaces, emphasizing the house's flexibility and dynamism.

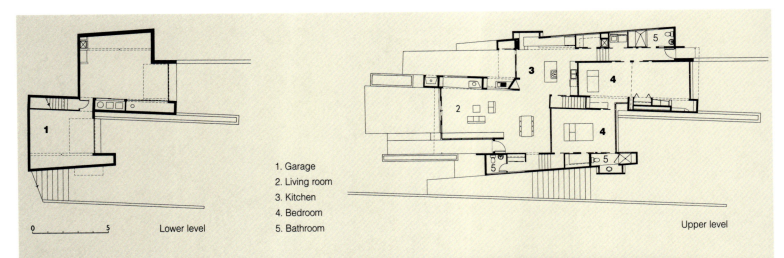

1. Garage
2. Living room
3. Kitchen
4. Bedroom
5. Bathroom

0   5   Lower level

Upper level

The challenge of this project was to create a contemporary house appropriate for the terrain, a rocky area alongside Lake Vermillion, Minnesota, that had a marvelous view of the lake and its surroundings. Creating a balance between tradition and innovative design is a problem common to many mountain projects, where the deep-rooted local architectural language collides with the formal ideas an undeveloped landscape can often inspire. Architect David Salmela's design succeeds in blending these concepts, while fulfilling the desires of the clients and their family.

The topography of the area and the specific location of the site reminds the client of the Swedish landscape of their ancestors. It was, in fact, the current owner's grandfather who built a farmhouse on the site when he emigrated from Sweden at the beginning of the twentieth century. During the long summers the present owner spent in the old house as a child, he developed a passion for boat building. Eventually, he and his wife decided to take early retirement to fulfill their dream of building a house. When the house was completed, they would then settle down to the business of building boats, a skill that had been passed down through the centuries by their ancestors.

This house, too, has inherited much from the past and from family tradition, but the project turns away from the architecture of yesteryear by keeping the composition modern. The house is conditioned by

DAVID SALMELA
☐ WILSON HOUSE
LAKE VERMILLION, MINNESOTA, USA.   PHOTOGRAPHY: PETER KERZE

the layout of visual centers, the maximization of natural light in the interior, and the subtle line arrangement, which is key to the architectural language. Notice, for example, the parallel spaces that flank the large living room, the most important place in the house, which determines the distribution of the other spaces. The main bedroom looks out to the west while the remaining bedrooms face the east. The conformity of the bedrooms is broken by the view of the rocky mountain outcrop and the deliberate changes introduced in the window arrangement. The living room is enclosed by Victorian-style shutters, which give it the appearance of a covered terrace, allowing it to serve as a transition between the interior of the house and the outdoors. In contrast, the patio takes on a less important role, containing and obscuring the view of the lake until the observer actually enters the house.

The interior contains areas for relaxing and gazing out at the landscape, framed by panoramic windows. The white walls and the sky is softened by the light wood tones of the floor, the handrails and the interior pergola over the living room. An extra touch of color is subtly provided by the gray and navy blue furniture and carpets.

☐ The most outstanding aspect of the project is the way it exists as a contemporary structure that has absorbed traditional tastes and qualities, making it the perfect place for someone to follow his grandfather's ways and spend the rest of his days building boats.

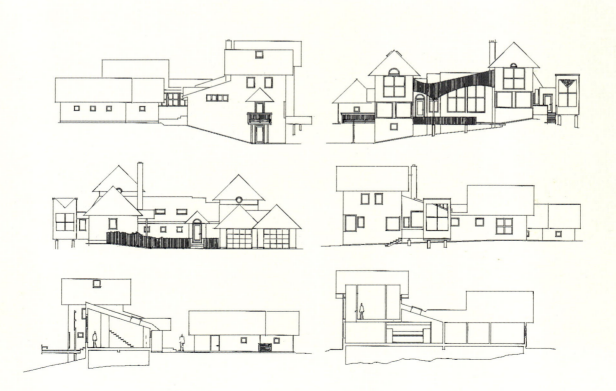

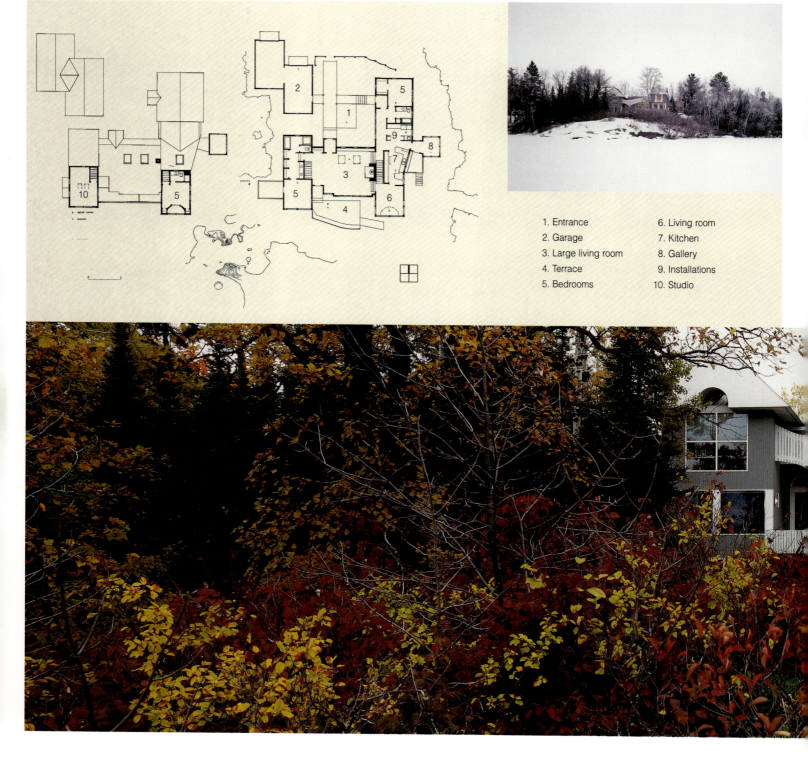

1. Entrance
2. Garage
3. Large living room
4. Terrace
5. Bedrooms
6. Living room
7. Kitchen
8. Gallery
9. Installations
10. Studio

The achievement and strength of this design come from its ability to combine the modern and traditional; the building has a classic appearance but at the same time is subject to a kind of spontaneous asymmetry. Echoes of the houses that predominate in the small towns in the region can be found in the high parallel forms and the A-shaped elements. The house maintains a pre-modern quality reminiscent of the days of the client's grandfather.

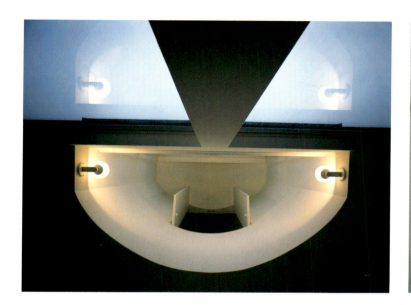

Generally, prefabricated houses seem thrown together without any thought to how they will look in situ, and rarely are they successfully transformed into structures that aspire to be more than basic, dull, utilitarian space. The enormous challenge this architect undertook was to design a prefabricated house that would go beyond the simple notion of a cabin and occupy its surroundings with the utmost delicacy and subtlety.

The basic concept was a family home that could be built quickly and easily in northern Italy's Tyrolean Alps. A detailed study of the site characteristics enabled the designer to create a structure suitable for the mountainous landscape and in keeping with the traditional architecture of the region.

Specifically, the building's spatial distribution and the formal approach used in the composition of each element convey these allusions to Alpine vernacular architecture. Note the enormously thick walls rising from the ground, the abundance of laminated wood surfaces, and the solid wood beams that support the wide roof section.

The structure is rectangular, composed along elemental lines, and topped with a roof reminiscent of the large-span structures typically seen on barns. The outside walls have a laminated wood skin, while shutters, also made of wood, filter the sunlight entering the house and unify the language of the building. The south face has been opened up by large windows that look out onto the spectacular landscape and ensure that as much sunshine as possible enters the house during the winter.

MATTEO THUN

HEIDI HOUSE

TYROLEAN ALPS, ITALY. 1998   PHOTOGRAPHY: EMILIO TREMOLADA, TIZIANO SARTORIO, JÜRGEN EHEIM

In addition, the structure is based on a tradition that, after a little reinterpretation to facilitate construction and accommodate a flexible system to allow for modifications, serves as the starting point for a variety of spatial ideas. Further, techniques to maximize energy efficiency have been incorporated. The very structure and its finishes are key components of the energy conservation systems. The construction is based on a three-dimensional reticular arrangement of solid Nordic pine columns and beams, fashioned from Alpine trees. The conditions in which these trees grow, exposed to the cold, snow, fierce heat, and dampness, mean that the wood is already perfectly weather-resistant when it arrives at the site, and there is no need for any sophisticated treatment. Another feature is the use of sound-absorbent material equivalent to a 16-inch-thick brick wall on a traditional house. This almost entirely eliminates the whistling and howling of the winds that often blow in these valleys. The structure, walls, roofs, and windows also provide excellent protection from the cold and minimize heat loss. The walls are thermally insulated with cork panels, which ensure that the house is not unduly affected by the sudden temperature drops characteristic of mountain climates. This feature, together with the house's solar panels, keeps energy consumption to a bare minimum. Also helping to reduce the consumption of energy is the great care that has been taken in designing the connections between the different living spaces.

☐ The design permits adaptation of the structure to each client's needs, achieving a wide variety of options with a basic concept.

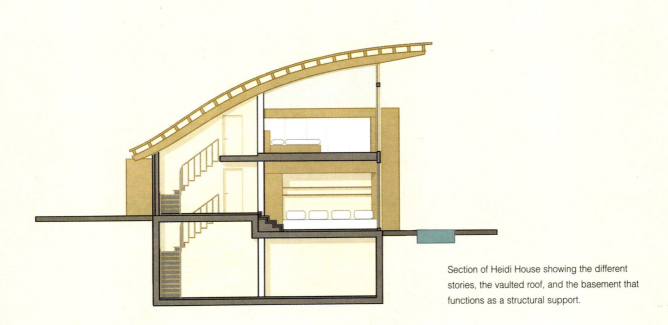

Section of Heidi House showing the different stories, the vaulted roof, and the basement that functions as a structural support.

☐ There is a vast difference between the appearance of this house and that of the prefabrication prototypes of the 1940s, which resembled barracks, huts, or caravans. The Heidi House, on the other hand, conveys the impression of a unique structure built for an individual client on a specific lot.

☐ Depending on specific needs, modules can be incorporated into the structure to provide either more bedrooms or larger common areas, all within a simple plan.

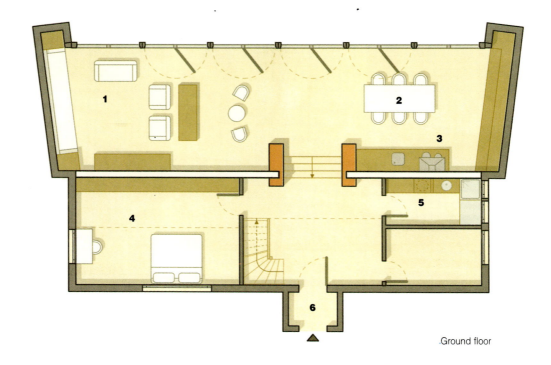

Ground floor

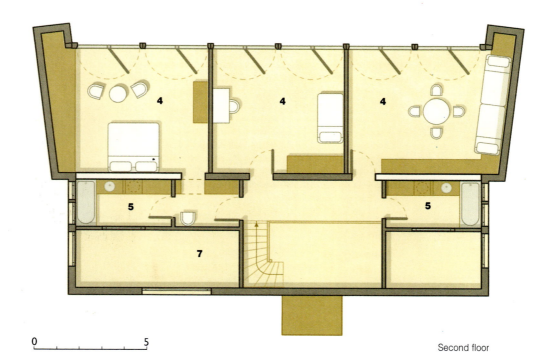

Second floor

1. Living room
2. Dining room
3. Kitchen
4. Bedroom
5. Bathroom
6. Entrance hall
7. Gallery

☐ The third story contains the bedrooms, all of which enjoy the same southern exposure as the living room and main bathroom. The small entrance hall leads to the point where all the access routes to the different living areas converge. Stairs lead to a guest room and small bathroom. On a slightly lower level is the extensive space that looks out through large windows onto the beautiful, mountainous landscape, which includes the living room, dining room, and kitchen.

This project is essentially concerned with correcting some unfortunate "improvements" inflicted on a mountain house that was originally a vacation home for a small family. The house is located a few yards from the Big Sucker, a rock-strewn river abounding in waterfalls, which flows through the site, less than a mile from Lake Superior in Duluth, Minnesota. Located about 300 feet above the lake, the site has a fantastic panoramic view of the vast expanse of water and the surrounding area. The original structure, which dates back to 1910, had undergone several badly planned and poorly executed reconstruction and enlargement projects. With the passing years, it became evident that these had weakened the structure and its foundations. When the current client commissioned the architect to draw up a plan to renovate the structure and make it suitable for himself and his family, it was seen as an excellent opportunity to recover the old house's original character. This became the project's starting point. Several factors influenced the design process: the history of the place and its traditional "mountain cabin" architecture, the aforementioned alterations, the family's Norwegian heritage and passion for Scandinavian design, and the need for space to display the client's enormous clock collection and for stables for his horses. However, the greatest single influence on the design process turned out to be the enormous interest the client and his family showed in architecture and the construction process. Building was carried out in eight separate phases over a period of five years. The completion of

DAVID SALMELA

LOKEN RESIDENCE

DULUTH, MINNESOTA, USA. 1995   PHOTOGRAPHY: PETER KERZE

each phase prompted vigorous discussion as to how the next stage should be implemented, focusing on progressive improvements in the project and reinforcement of the original design concepts. This led to the incorporation of features such as soundproofed areas, the restoration of the old house, and the removal of certain sections that were beyond repair. The result was a design that made better use of the physical location and the existing structures, creating a cozy dwelling that functioned as a unified whole. In general, the project attempted to create an architectural language suitable for a new building— a symbolic, rural language respectful of the integrity and simplicity of the original structure. The whole family contributed ideas for the design, and the result was an array of features that stand alone but at the same time are consistent within the overall project: an example of family harmony transposed into architecture. Patios and vistas were developed from both the old and the new structures, while sheltered garden spaces were defined through rock walls, cultivated areas, and colored surfaces. The original house was completely redesigned. The architect incorporated a tower containing the library and family living space whose scale is respectful of the preexisting structure. The family home was complemented by the addition of a bathhouse and horse barn.

☐ Wood, the predominant material for both the exterior and interior, has been used in a way that exploits its plastic qualities to the maximum. In this project, the traditional layout of the mountain cabin, a very common structure in this region, has been reinterpreted to create clean, simple interior spaces. The exterior, in contrast, employs a varied yet formal approach that leads to its incorporation, piece by piece, into the landscape.

1. Entrance   2. Living room   3. Dining room   4. Kitchen   5. TV room
6. Garage   7. Stables   8. Bedrooms   9. Studio   10. Loft

Lower level

Upper level

☐ The spatial layout of the home and its placement of windows allow for a direct relationship with the surrounding landscape.

☐ The interior features a series of intimate, welcoming spaces, due to a lighting arrangement that brings out the tone and luster of the wood. The same material predominates in the furniture and in some of the decorative pieces, generating a certain unity of form.

On the upper floor of the house, maximum use has been made of the space beneath the sloping roof surfaces, in keeping with traditional cabin design, although the pentagonal attic space within provides a modern touch.

The narrow passes in the mountains behind Brisbane, Australia, are mysterious, almost magical, places. They are luxuriantly verdant reminders of what the original landscape in this region was like before development slowly ate away at the terrain. The wild and densely wooded lot on which Rosebery House is built presented difficulties for the architects. The narrow canyon reaches its steepest point toward the north, which would be the optimum direction for a house to be facing, since in the southern hemisphere the light and the warmth come from the north. In addition, the ground's water level required the structure to be raised above the surface, at considerable cost. The architects were faced with the challenge of building with a limited budget on a difficult site without destroying the landscape's inherent qualities. After completing an exhaustive study of the land and the surrounding environment, they designed a slender structure along a north–south axis. This was intended to emphasize the length of the narrow pass and show it as the connector of the hill and the river. The house is located at one end of the site, facing away from the neighboring buildings and looking westward toward the trees. This gives it more privacy and a certain referential scale. One of the priorities of the project was to diffuse the warm northern light into the darkest area, beneath the tree canopies. This was achieved by designing the house in three pavilion sections, inter-connected by semi-covered platform walkways. This arrangement, together with the extensive use of large windows, considerably increases the

BRIT ANDRESEN & PETER O'GORMAN
ROSEBERY HOUSE
BRISBANE, AUSTRALIA. 1997   PHOTOGRAPHY: JOHN LINKINS AND BRIT ANDRESEN

natural interior light, while translucent sections along the roof, with slatted blinds made of wood, simulate the effect of light filtering through the leaves of the trees. The wooden pillars supporting the facade provide a vertical rhythm that echoes the lines of the trees in the nearby woods. The exterior walls vary between partially opaque (plywood and cement fiber) areas and transparent, glassed-in sections. Hard eucalyptus wood is used for both the structure and the delicate detailing, which harmonizes with the pattern created by the branches of the bushes. In the center of the west-facing wall, there is a tall opening that marks the entrance to the house. This aperture is enclosed by a semitransparent wooden screen, which serves as a veil, partially concealing the structure and obscuring its scale, so as not to detract from the rugged grandeur of the pass. To enhance this effect, plants have been trained up the screen, so the boundary between nature and man-made construction fades. Behind this entrance screen are the three pavilion sections, which make up the house. The central one is the most public, containing the kitchen, dining room, laundry, and study. The section to the north has the bedrooms with their bathrooms, while the third section is a quiet living space with a fireplace. This room, a kind of refuge above the trees, enjoys beautiful views of the forest and river.

☐ The drawing clearly shows the house and its specific location, which architects Andresen & O'Gorman used to such advantage. Their project was based on respect for nature—building within the landscape without negatively affecting it.

☐ This project gave the architects the opportunity to explore the relationship between landscape and construction, while requiring particular attention to the intermediate spaces and the use of transparency and occlusion.

☐ This problematic but magnificent site is part of a narrow pass that stretches to the Brisbane River. The steep gradient and the lush forest make the land difficult to work on, but its wonder and charm more than compensate. The interior spaces connect with the adjacent forest so that the boundary between construction and nature becomes unnoticeable.

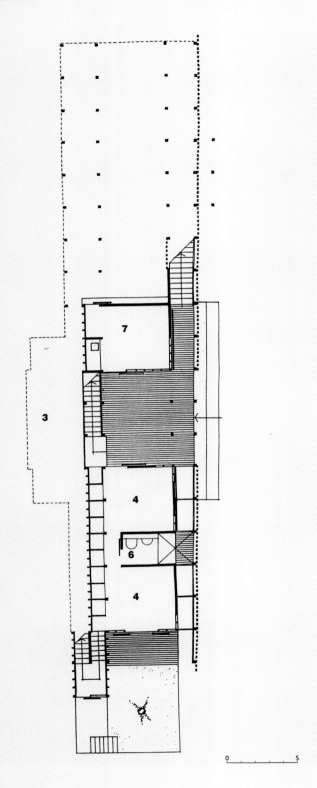

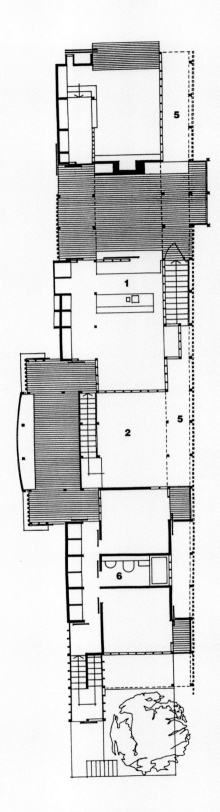

1. Kitchen
2. Entrance
3. Terraces
4. Bedroom
5. Balconies
6. Bathroom
7. Study

0   5

☐ The structure rests on a support system of wooden beams and pillars. The terraces and balconies are partially covered by eucalyptus wood slats that shade the house from the heat of the sun, which can be fierce in these latitudes. The platforms connecting the different sections of the house play an important role, as they directly relate to the surrounding environment.

☐ Functionally, the house is arranged in three pavilion sections that are connected by means of walkways or partially covered terraces. The terraces provide protection from the heat of the sun and are ambiguous spaces where the dividing line between interior and exterior becomes unclear. The lower level has a small apartment for guests or teenagers who demand more independence.

The cabin is a simple structure—with a rectangular ground plan and a gable roof—integrated into the Masía Masnou complex in the heart of the natural park in the volcanic area of La Garrotxa, Girona, Spain. Commissioned as a dwelling, its plan has a formal clarity, which led the architects to highlight the original characteristics. The construction employed a kind of masonry that combined the local volcanic stone with lime mortar. On the first floor, however, the walls are made of a different material: ceramic bricks laid out in a latticework arrangement, providing excellent ventilation. An external stairway mounted on the wall allows access to the upper floors. The main alteration to the existing structure consisted of adding a perforated steel section, resting on a volume of similar dimensions, hidden beneath the main level behind the stone walls.

Three stories sit atop the simple but highly effective base. This supporting structure is independent from the original walls and leaves lateral strips extending on the north and south sides. These strips are covered with movable laminated glass sheets that act as skylights for the lower story. The brick sections on the first level are broken by large windows, which provide ample light for the living room.

Below, a mezzanine contains the kitchen and dining room, while another, on a higher level, accommodates the bedrooms. Both the guest rooms and the garage are on the ground floor, and there is direct

JORDI HIDALGO AND DANIELA HARTMANN
☐ # CABIN AT MASÍA MASNOU
LES PRESES, GIRONA, SPAIN   PHOTOGRAPHY: EUGENI PONS

access from the adjacent lawn. An external stairway runs up to the main entrance of the house and leads through a hall to the main staircase, which connects all the stories. The open area provided by the central stairway helps create a spatial and visual continuity that highlights the volumetric qualities of the house.

One of the most important design features in this architecturally integrated effect is the use of perforated, rusty iron sheeting, which acts as a kind of reference to the original enclosure while containing a clearly contemporary space. A certain intimacy is achieved by the fact that the sheeting is virtually opaque from the exterior but transparent from inside. The positioning of this partly fixed, partly movable encircling layer creates a kind of gallery above the skylight and alters the ultimate expression of the building. Thus, according to the lighting conditions and the observer's point of view, the house may appear as either a closed block of heavy material, such as stone, or a semi-transparent steel box resting on an empty glass expanse. This duality unites the cabin's architectural past with the contemporary formal language employed in the construction.

☐ The architects' objective was to create a building that demonstrated conceptual clarity while maximizing the perceptive sensations available from the interior.

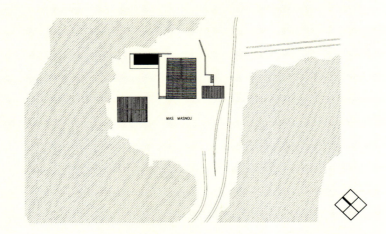

MAS MASNOU

☐ The supporting structure is a traditional wood truss-rafter arrangement which holds the gable
   roof and rests on a lattice of beams and metal pillars that underpins the new enclosures.

☐ The kitchen furniture was designed exclusively for the house. The cabinets employ
   transparent and translucent glass, allowing the utensils and china to be seen.

☐ A light, transparent design was used for the stairway to accentuate its architectural space and establish a visual relationship among all areas within the house.

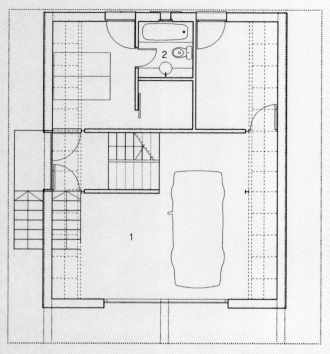

Ground floor

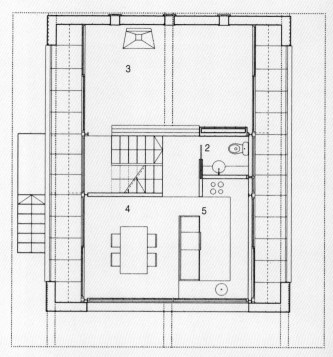

Second floor

0   5

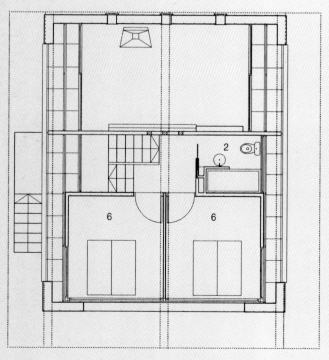

Third floor

1. Garage
2. Bathrooms
3. Living room
4. Dining room
5. Kitchen
6. Bedrooms

☐ The elevations reveal the formal simplicity of the project. A few well-founded decisions have produced highly original results—a structure that respects both the environment and the architecture of the original building.

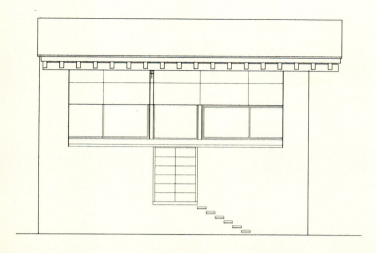

Southwest facade

Southeast facade

□ The stairway, located in the central service and distribution area, divides the ground plan into two equal parts on different levels. Starting from the bottom are the garage, guest rooms, dining room and kitchen, living room, and bedrooms.

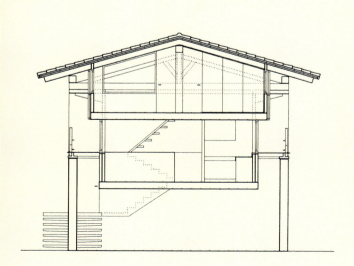

Transversal section

□ The perforated steel sheet enclosure and delicate handrails create an interesting contrast, while transparency and reflection combine to provide different views of the leafy surroundings.

The simple structure of this summer house perfectly reflects the atmosphere of peace and calm that pervades these hills in Risor, in southern Norway. It also exemplifies an architecture introduced into the landscape with the utmost delicacy. Enormous care was taken, not only to ensure that the various environmental features were respected, but also to integrate each one into the design itself. This was possible because of the sensitive approach taken by the architect and the clients toward the environment, and the sophisticated architectural means that were employed during the course of the project.

It should also be mentioned that the site is an outstanding choice for development, since it typifies the region's landscape–rocky hills and sparse pine forests abounding in cozy nooks and sheltered spots. In addition, while the vicinity is dominated by enormous stone surfaces, there are seven hardy old pine trees in the most open space on the lot. Another attractive feature of the site is its mountainside location near the coast, which provides a fantastic panoramic view of the sea.

For 25 years, the clients had been spending their summers in a cabin on the site. While enjoying and admiring the fine landscape, they came up with the idea of subtly adding another building. Eventually, they did, and the original building is used primarily by the clients' children and grandchildren.

The site's natural environmental features are influenced in the design. The clients were particularly fond of the old pine trees and as a result, they built the house right in their midst. The site was carefully surveyed using computerized levelling instruments to create an extremely precise plan of the land and the trees. The structure's foundations

CARL VIGO HØLMEBAKK

☐ SUMMER HOUSE

NORTHWOODS, MINNESOTA, USA. 1998   PHOTOGRAPHY: PETER KERZE

consist of a specially designed, adjustable arrangement of concrete pillars, whose placement was determined by the size and location of the main wooden beams. To avoid damaging the pine's root system, each pillar was driven into the ground in a specific direction. More than 30 such pillars were installed without destroying any roots. The entire array of columns and laminated wooden beams was precut and pre-shaped by the carpenter. Steel was used to construct the skeletal structure of prefabricated sections and the points where these join the foundation. The walls, windows, and doors were incorporated later, leaving the columns visible from both the interior and exterior.

The position of the tree trunks and branches determined the size and shape of the building. The roof sections are rranged at heights between approximately 6 1/2 and 8 1/2 feet. Continuous onsite checks were made to fine-tune the building's spatial features, such as the organization of the walls, glass panels, and windows. Occasionally, windows were even incorporated during the actual process of framework construction. In spite of the building's relatively limited floor space (approximately 600 square feet), it seems spacious, since the interior extends outward by means of terraces, stairways, and open patios. During most of the day, the wooden terrace and the open expanse of rock on the west side of the house function as the main living room. In addition, this partly natural, partly constructed space has been provided with features, such as a barbecue pit and raised herb garden, that effectively bring the kitchen outside.

☐ The Norwegian summer is short and, possibly as a result, very beautiful. Within this context, a summer house can be regarded as an architectural short story—a building project that demands the utmost precision and intensity of expression despite the fact that the result is a space for pleasure and relaxation.

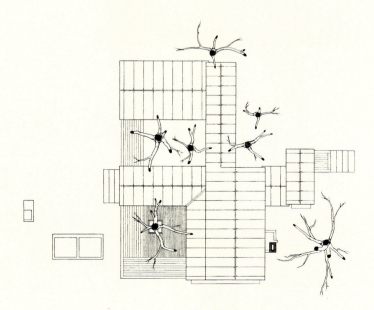

□ Different woods were used to meet construction requirements: Norwegian pine, spruce, and
oak. Larch from Siberia was also used. All of the wood was specially treated to make it
resistant to aging and the cold, humid climate.

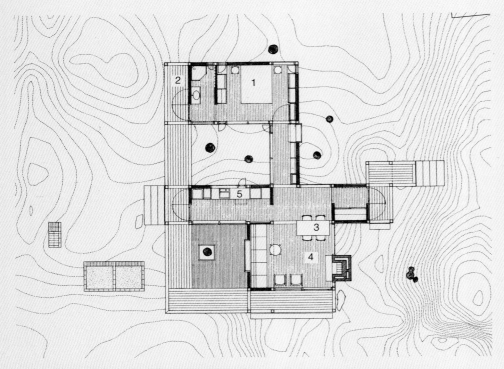

1. Bedroom
2. Bathroom
3. Dining room
4. Living room
5. Kitchen

☐ The external surfaces were treated with oil; the roof sections (at a five-degree slope)
were covered with galvanized iron sheeting.

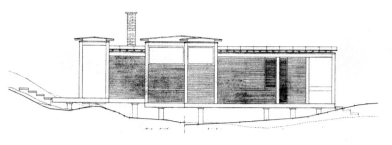

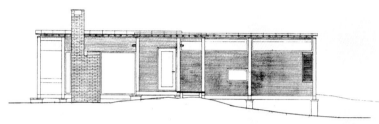

☐ The elevations show the subtlety with which the house was introduced into the rocky landscape. The uneven land surface was dealt with by using a flat platform supported by pillars.

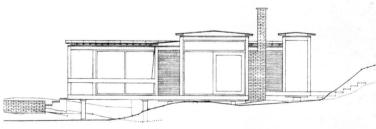

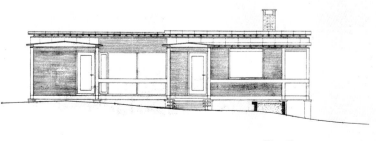

Elevations

This plan for a duplex house on the outskirts of Basel, Switzerland, exemplifies the close interplay that can be created between site and structure, so that a large space can be subtly incorporated into the landscape. In addition, the numerous peculiarities of the building lot made the designer think about different options, since conventional principles of sequence and levels (e.g., rows of houses or blocks of apartments) could not be employed here.

The land extends lengthwise toward the access road to the west. The remaining perimeter is defined by dense vegetation on the adjacent properties, creating an open-space effect. The site has an unusual dynamism that is accented by its proportions and by a row of old fruit trees, an evocative reminder of the predominantly agrarian nature of the region. The identically sized homes rest on a concrete base that enables the structure to overcome the gradient and reach up to the hill. The interlaced structure is difficult to interpret, since from the outside it appears to be a single dwelling instead of a duplex. The complex overlapping organization of the two homes is more than justified by the fact that all inhabitants can enjoy the site's different orientations as well as the direct contact between the first floor and the external environment. Both homes benefit from the magnificent panoramic views of the Rhine and the Vosges valleys, in addition to the serenity of the neighbouring gardens and

HARRY GUGGER

☐ TWO-FAMILY DUPLEX

BASEL, SWITZERLAND. 1996   PHOTOGRAPHY: MARGHERITA SPILUTTINI

the dense foliage. Two intersecting stairways adjacent to the north face of the building link the two levels of the houses and serve as a corridor, thereby elegantly minimizing the circulation area. The staircases extend to the very top of the building, providing an unexpected impression of opulence and, more concretely, a perception of the height and the depth of the building as a whole, producing the sensation of being in a whole house, and not just in a part of one. There is a definite demarcation between the land and the abstract, incorruptible appearance of the building. The outcome is a relationship between the interior and the exterior that occurs exclusively through the windows. Wooden slats also serve as screens for the large sliding windows, which are set between this level and the prefabricated structure. Closed, the windows look fixed and frameless; open, they simply disappear. Reducing the windows to simple perforations in the building's skin expresses the idea of a direct link between the existing medium and the world that goes on within the house.

☐ The open space around the house has not been turned into a typical suburban garden. Instead, it has been interpreted as a landscape within itself, thus conserving the original dimensions and nature of the site.

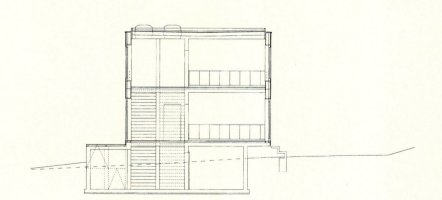

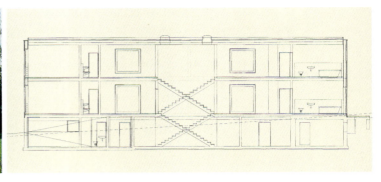

☐ The semi-wilderness of the surrounding area convinced the architect,
Harry Gugger, to build and position the house as if it were a solitary
feature that had strayed onto the landscape.

☐ The relationship with the environment is even clearer when seen from the interior. The windows are a series of glazed squares that not only reflect the natural world but draw it into the very interior of the space. When the windows are open, the rooms are transformed into veritable loggias. The entrances are conceived in the same way, looking on to a corridor of wooden slats that convert the base of the building into a deck. This combination of restrained language and spareness of elements creates a strong bond between landscape and architecture.

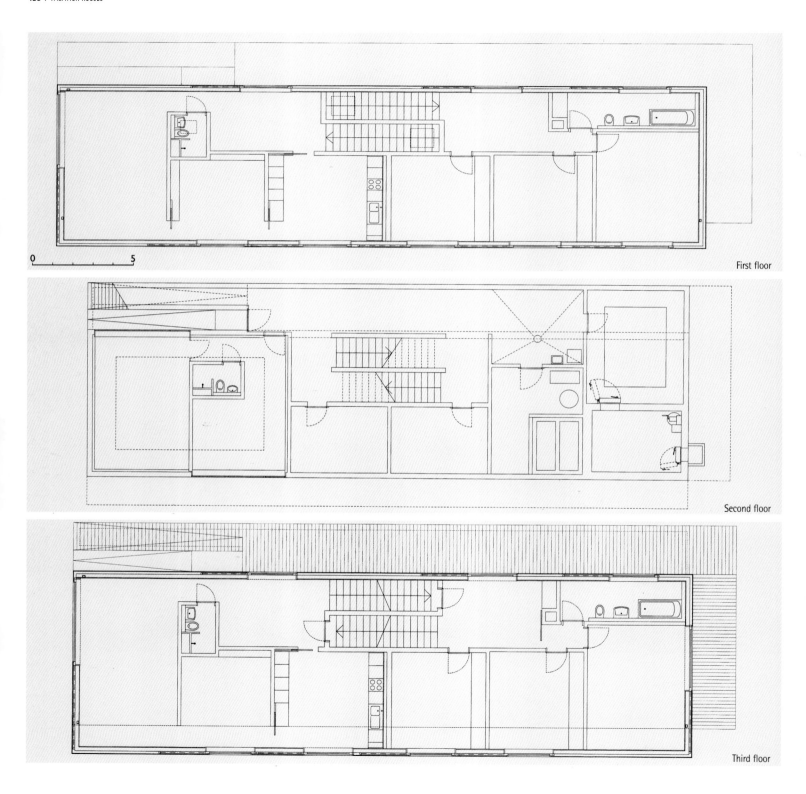

First floor

0   5

Second floor

Third floor

☐ The surfaces of the exterior walls are elegant in formal appearance but with a rough finish that contrasts with the fineness of the glazed surfaces.

☐ In these latitudes, there is no need for extensive protection from the sun's rays, so the windows can be large, clean expanses without slats or blinds.

The location gives the house wonderful views of the surrounding countryside. All of the large windows look out onto the garden, providing the interior with abundant natural light and pleasant views of the surrounding vegetation.

The principal influence on this project's design was the need for two distinct residences for very different clients, but viewed as a unit employing the same architectural expression. This stemmed from the family ties between the two clients and the desire to impact the landscape as economically and subtly as possible. The plan was to design one home for a single man and another smaller home for his mother, who visits periodically throughout the year. Each house has two bedrooms each with a bathroom, a kitchen, and a living room. The main house also has a room for the client's eight labradors and a cockatoo, as well as a garage for a collection of six cars. The challenge was to give each of the residences its own character, style, and space while making them complementary—unique but harmonious.

The site is near Pound Ridge in New York State, just below the top of a mountain, on a forested, west-facing slope between two rocky rises that frame the landscape. It can be reached by car only from the upper part of the hill, while the best lake views are lower down. Despite the site's peculiarities, both homes have the same accessibility, natural light, and views and are similarly integrated into the surroundings. From their privileged location, there are excellent lake and valley views with easy motor access from above.

Each house has its own characteristics and distinguishing details, although the language is the same. The project is divided

FRANK LUPO AND DANIEL ROWEN

BACH HOUSE

POUND RIDGE, NEW YORK, USA. 1996   PHOTOGRAPHY: MICHAEL MORAN

into two side-by-side structures with different orientations. The mother's house, slightly higher up, is basically a cube topped by a vaulted roof. In contrast, the son's house, which is perpendicular, runs down the mountainside toward the pond. A series of terraces, playing with and breaking down the houses' cubic elements, leads into the natural landscape.

Between the two houses, a shared terrace frames the landscape and visually connects the pond and the mountain. The terrace acts as a buffer between the mother's and son's houses. By defining and separating the relationship between landscape and nature, it unites the entire project. There is tension in the space, where separation and connection coexist. The terrace is protected by the roof of the mother's house, which projects over it. The natural stone and wide openings help this space, which is accessible from both houses, blend into the scenery.

Inside the houses, each room has a unique character. In both houses, the larger space, including the living areas below and the main bedrooms above, is lower and enjoys panoramic views. The smaller space, on the mountainside, contains the stairs, kitchen, and service areas.

☐ The houses are halfway between the mountaintop and a pond, with a panoramic view of the valley. The project blends into the landscape.

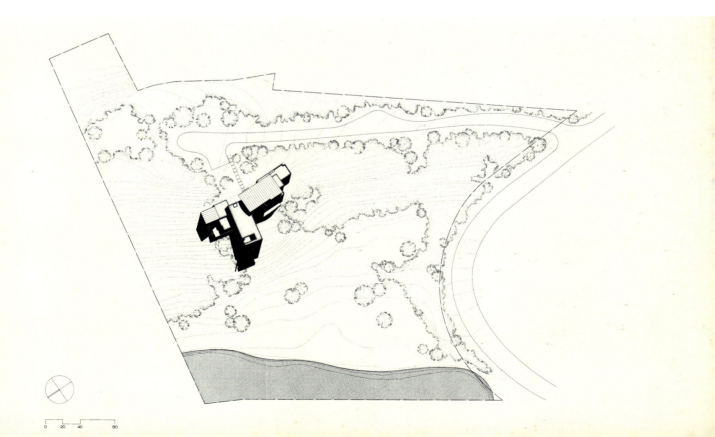

0   20   40   80

☐ In accordance with the simple, basic geometric elements embodied in the design, the materials used inside and outside are minimized. The concrete walls and the metal roof and handrailing give the houses a distinctive monochrome quality and clear lines.

☐ The project employs contrasting materials. Inside, concrete and metal predominate; outside, the natural stone in the common areas blends with the countryside.

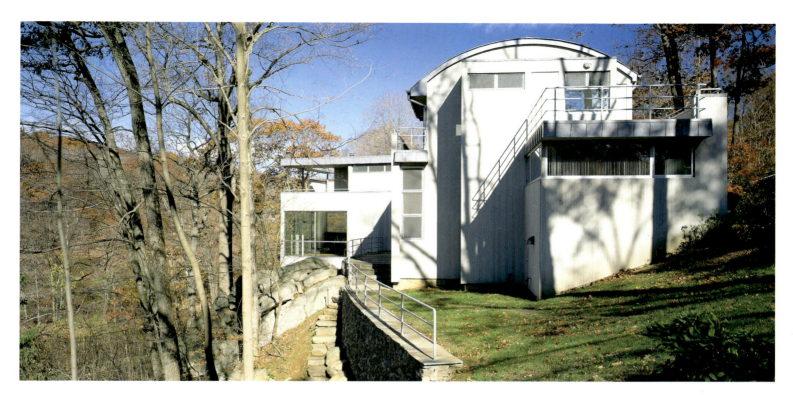

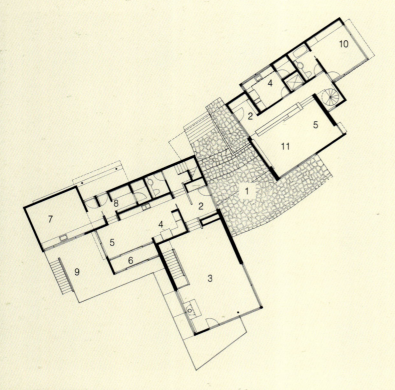

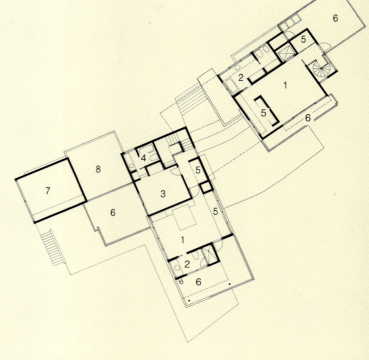

Ground floor

1. Terrace
2. Entrance
3. Living room
4. Kitchen
5. Dining room
6. Gallery
7. Studio
8. Bathroom
9. Terrace
10. Guest bedrooms
11. Living room

Second level

1. Main bedroom
2. Main bedroom
3. Guest bedroom
4. Guest bedroom
5. Storage
6. Terrace
7. Studio
8. Roof

0   5

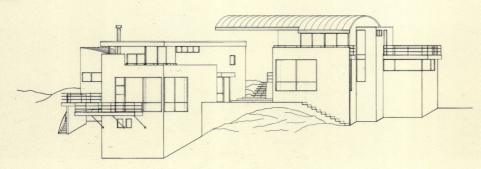

Minimalism, in the context of this project, can be defined as a way of building that affects the natural surroundings as little as possible. It is the most appropriate language for establishing a dialogue with the landscape. This approximately 1,184-square-foot house, located in the Yamanaka Mountains of Japan, has the appearance of an autonomous unit set off from the lush surrounding vegetation. The priority for Japanese architect Shigeru Ban was a house that would express an extreme simplicity. Accordingly, he designed the building around a series of partitions, prefabricated units occupying the entire height of the building, which perform a structural role and define the interior space. In contrast to conventional wood construction, these units can be industrially mass-produced, ensuring their quality and homogeneity. Another advantage of the units, which function as both pieces of furniture and as structural elements, is a significant reduction in materials, manpower, and construction time. This, of course, results in considerable savings in project costs. The furniture units used in the house

SHIGERU BAN

□ FURNITURE HOUSE

YAMANAKA MOUNTAINS, JAPAN. 1998   PHOTOGRAPHY: HIROYUKI HIRAI

are nearly 8 feet high and 3 feet wide. Their depth, which is determined by their function, varies between 17 inches for bookcases and 27 inches for general storage units or shelving. Arranged according to the structure and composition of the rooms, they add vertical and horizontal tension to the plan and strengthen the dynamic of the interior space. It is also much easier to transport this prefabricated furniture than conventional construction materials, since an entire prefabricated unit weighs approximately 176 pounds, and can therefore be easily handled and moved by one person. In addition, these pieces are self-supporting, which facilitates assembly. Six strips of structural furniture are used as dividers, creating different living areas inside one continuous space. The architect simply places the pieces in such a way that they direct all movement and vision outward, toward a large platform, while the large screens (which slide open and shut on rails embedded in the floor and roof) play their part by connecting the interior space with the surrounding landscape.

☐ The axonometric perspective clearly shows the structural organization of the house, a latticework of metal pillars and other vertical elements supporting an arrangement of beams. The rear wall gives the structure horizontal rigidity.

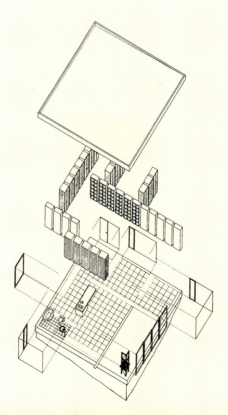

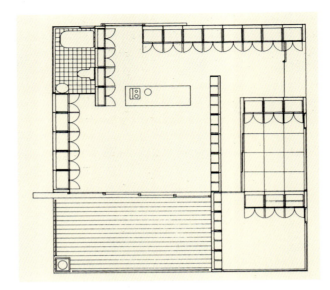

☐ Shigeru Ban, internationally known for his ephemeral constructions in Kobe (using cardboard
cylinders as structural supports), has returned to the same principles in this project but has
extended them into a more radical and permanent design.

☐ The building calls to mind constructions by Kamo no Chomei, the twelfth century architect who built structures in sections that could be taken apart and reassembled in a different way. Shigeru Ban's design is a modern, experimental reinterpretation of the classic tradition of Japanese architecture.

☐ The elegant interior, reminiscent of the first houses of Mies van der Rohe, is the result of a highly intelligent distribution of space that avoids clear differentiations among the functions of the dwelling. The demarcation between circulation routes and living spaces, or between interior and exterior, is either virtually nonexistent or suggested in a very subtle way.

One of the principal requirements of any building project is defining the relationship between the structure and the surroundings. For this venture, the house had to be built on the slopes of Mount Worcester, a rocky mountain covered by maples, beeches, and firs, with breathtaking views typical of Stowe, Vermont. With dramatic temperature changes, abundant rainfall and snowfall, and the colors and winds of all seasons, the area offers architects and builders great opportunities and as many potential pitfalls.

The clients, a couple with grown children, were seeking a second residence with four guest bedrooms, living quarters for a housekeeper, a three-car garage, a granary, a garden house, and a tennis court. With the seductive landscape as a backdrop, the architect had to fit this into 6,450 square feet.

Working in collaboration with landscape architect Dan Kiley, Peter Rose grouped together the main structures—living quarters, guest area, granary, and garage— at a spot midway up the mountain, overlooking a pond and meadow, where the slope allowed construction with little disturbance of the soil. The four buildings surround a patio, which is the entrance to the complex. Mount Mansfield can be seen in the distance.

A path through the forest leads to the house. As one ascends, the lushness subsides and parts of the complex come into view. Finally one reaches the patio, where American beech trees have been planted to lend homogeneity to the project.

The different elements have been laid out to maximize the panoramic views and take advantage of the cool summer breezes while providing protection from the harsh winter winds. Utmost advantage is taken of

THE OFFICE OF PETER ROSE

☐ A HOUSE IN VERMONT

STOWE, VERMONT, USA. 1997   PHOTOGRAPHY: BRIAN VANDEN BRINK

the sunlight, although there is ample shade for the hot season.

Spread beneath sloping roofs, the house blends intimately with its surroundings. The glass openings are strategically positioned to accentuate this closeness, while the project is further integrated into the landscape through the use of local materials and construction systems in tune with the natural environment.

In building the main living quarters and guest rooms, the architects used a wide variety of materials: brick, stone, rock, wood, concrete slabs, steel, aluminum, glass, and plaster. This diversity demonstrates their efforts to get the most out of traditional construction while improving it with new components. Concrete slabs, for example, are uncommon in rural New England construction. They were included after Rose investigated the possible use of prefabricated units.

Inside, the same enthusiasm for experimentation led to the use of distinctive elements, making each room unique, although uniformly severe. Good examples are the different window types, which combine steel, aluminum, and glass, and the integrated lighting system in the kitchen.

Peter Rose is known for scrupulousness and for championing enduring architecture. In a culture increasingly dominated by ephemera and appearance, he believes in the construction of substantive, durable buildings. As he has said, "Anything that costs as much as architecture costs, and which changes as many places as architecture does, must be able to grow old gracefully."

☐ Located on the west slope of Mount Worcester, the project includes a concrete block living area with a guest wing made of metal and wood. Both are covered by copper-paneled roofs.

☐ The site has stunning views. In the foreground are a pond and meadow. In the distance, Mount Mansfield, the highest peak in Vermont, can be seen.

☐ Although the materials used are not traditional to the architecture of the area, the double-pitched gable roofs echo the design of the neighboring buildings.

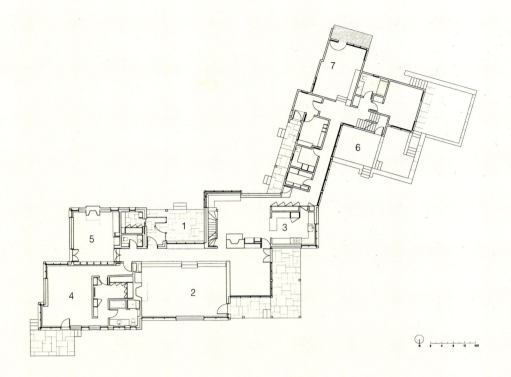

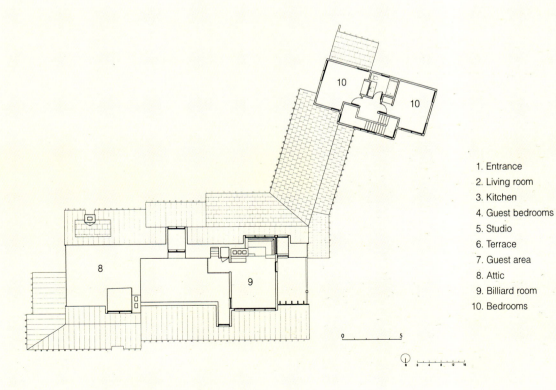

1. Entrance
2. Living room
3. Kitchen
4. Guest bedrooms
5. Studio
6. Terrace
7. Guest area
8. Attic
9. Billiard room
10. Bedrooms

This house is the culmination of artist Michael Singer's exploration, begun in the 1970s, of the interaction between structures and the natural environment. His first works were ephemeral, made of bamboo, autumnal trees, or various types of wood lightly poised on the ground or, sometimes, emerging from the water. Later, he began incorporating heavier materials, especially concrete. His work became more practical and structural, while testing the boundaries between art and architecture, and landscape and construction. After collaborating with various architectural teams on landscape projects and the design of some small pavilions, Singer consolidated his ideas on architectural language with this mountain house.

The building site, near Brattleboro, Vermont, was carefully chosen by the client to meet his special requirements. Although it is in a forested area, the village is only a short walk away. The natural clearing meant that no trees had to be cut. In addition, there are fine views to the south and abundant light, which brightens and warms the interior of the dwelling. The concept was simple, for the client lives austerely, has little furniture, rarely cooks, and needs little storage space. What he did need, as a devotee of folk-dancing, was a large practice space and an evocative atmosphere for inspiration.

From the outset, Singer realized that this architectural project and a large sculpture he was working on in his studio were

MICHAEL SINGER

☐ PARKER-HUBER HOUSE

BRATTLEBORO, VERMONT, USA. 1998 PHOTOGRAPHY: DAVID STANSBURY

connected. Like his other works, this piece involved sealing, layering, and materiality.

As the design and construction of the house progressed, the projects became more complementary, feeding off one another. For example, he introduced a protective element that clearly divided the house and street. In his studio, the artist made a richly textured screen of concrete panels to mark the frontier between public and private. This facade, typical of his other designs, incorporates wooden shapes into the reinforced concrete. As a kind of visual echo, those shapes were molded in concrete, producing an intricate dialogue between the materials. The screen is not part of the building's structure. Secured to concrete slabs outside the house, it sets off the wooden building. Over time, indigenous creeping plants will give the front of the house a lush green color. This vegetation heightens intimacy and softens the transition from outside to inside.

The interior centers around a two-story living room with magnificent views to the east and south. A wooden dance floor under the open beams occupies most of the space. Cushions are scattered about for resting. The private spaces—kitchen, bathroom, and sleeping and working quarters—occupy the sides of the building, where the design is somewhat more solid.

□ The use and arrangement of selected materials has created a framework that harmonizes with the nearby landscape.

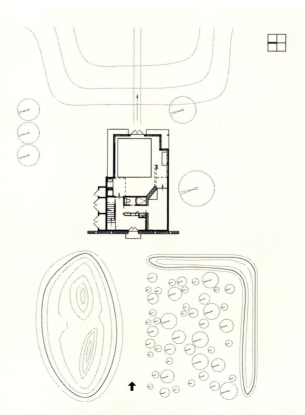

☐ On the main level, dark coloring has been applied to the concrete flooring. The surface is warmer in the bedroom. The white walls provide balance and contrast. A bedroom and studio on the upper floor accentuate the simplicity of the first floor and provide flexibility.

This house is located in a resort area at the foot of Mount Tateshina in Nagano, Japan. The terrain slopes gently toward the southwest, and a forest surrounds the lot.

As Iida himself explains, a vacation home is not subject to the same hierarchies as a primary residence. The relationships among the residents are more relaxed. Different activities can often take place in the same location, since they do not require as much isolation and concentration. Finally, there is generally a closer relationship with nature, since vacationers usually want to enjoy outdoor life. As a result, many of the most innovative and compelling architectural works are vacation homes, since the owners' needs and desires require more open space and permit a less conventional layout.

Iida's project proceeds from a basic design of two slightly displaced, parallel rectangular structures. They are set along the slope of the land with access from above. From the vestibule, a ramp descends along the natural slope of the hill, leading the visitor to the living room and large wooden patio at the other end. The ramp then continues until it disappears into the forest.

A second ramp leads up from the vestibule to the neighboring building. Here, an unusually open bath with panoramic views of the forest provides a perfect spot for hours of relaxation. An exterior staircase leads from the contiguous patio to the wooden deck on the ground floor.

IIDA ARCHISHIP STUDIO
☐ HOUSE IN TATESHINA

TATESHINA, NAGANO, JAPAN. 1995   PHOTOGRAPHY: KOUMEI TANAKA

The house is arranged on this circuit, which links the two floors and the interior to the patios. As in Iida's other projects, the "O" Residence, the itinerary around the house, is the axis that determines the distribution and design of the spaces.

Architecture can ignore time and be based on fixed, independent images. This is only possible, however, when it takes into account its occupants' tempos, pauses, speeds, and agendas. Only then can it transcend constructive logic, functional room arrangements, and purely visual and physical attributes, and become a harmonious construction, inviting those who inhabit it to experience space in a richer, more complete, and less arbitrary way.

The largest area contains the vestibule, tatami room, dining room, and living room. Here, the various spaces are terraced according to the slope of the terrain and the ramp. It is effectively one large two-story room with closed side walls, open at the front and back. At each end, a patio links the interior with the forest.

Seen in this light, Yoshihiko Iida's project might be considered the simplest construction possible—little more than a couple of walls and a roof situated along one of the paths crossing the mountain, providing a modest refuge for sleeping and bathing.

☐ So that the house blends into the tones of the surrounding forest, the most widely used material in the interior and exterior is wood.

☐ There is a large wooden platform in front of the house, which is divided into different levels, almost like a public square. This outdoor space features a double-height porch and a sculpture-like staircase.

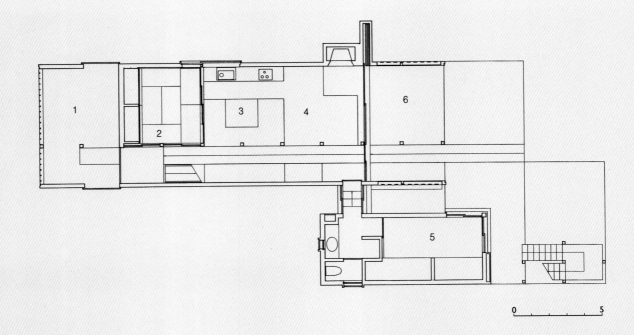

Ground floor

1. Entrance
2. Tatami room
3. Dining room
4. Living room
5. Bedroom
6. Terrace

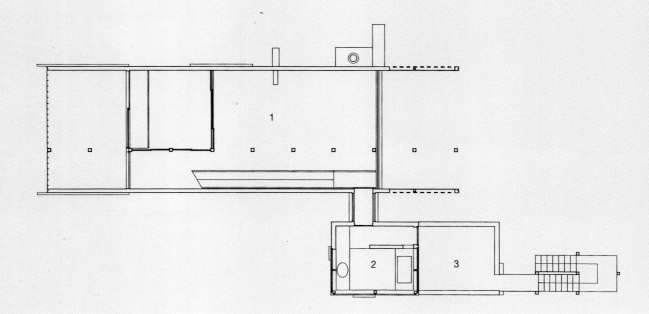

Second floor

1. Empty space
2. Bathroom
3. Terrace

0 ————————— 5

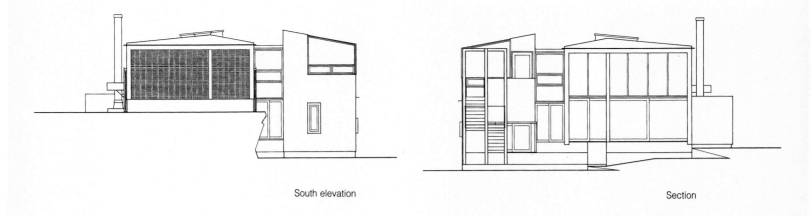

South elevation

Section

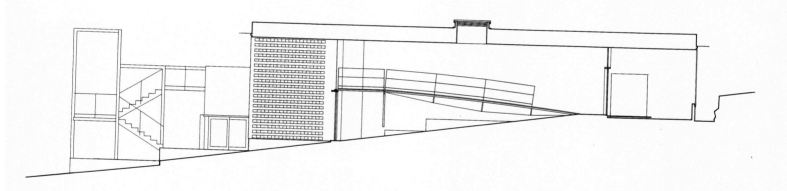

Longitudinal section

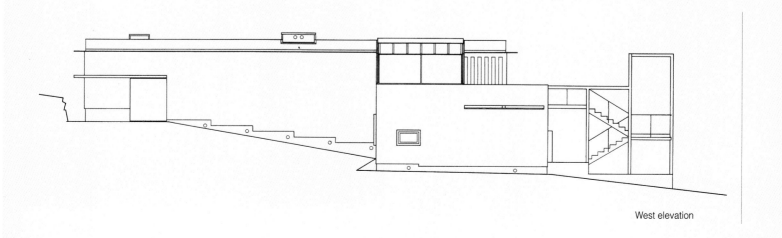

West elevation

☐ The space has an extraordinarily simple and contained image due to the extensive use of wood, for both the furniture and the wall paneling, and the simple geometry.
The ramps create a circular walkway through the house that begins in the forest, crosses the residence, and disappears again in the trees.

☐ The longitudinal section shows the elements, including two ramps and a stairway, that determine the flow and organization of the house's different levels.

Finally, after years of architectural design errors that sometimes damaged the landscape beyond repair, a new concept of architecture is emerging. This concept, with far more respect for the natural environment, is ideal for creating harmony between a structure and the geographical features of its building site.

One's first impression of Burkhardt House in Bridgman, Michigan, is that it affords protection from the immense space around it—a kind of architectural identity that exists in contrast to the chaos of nature. The house was conceived as a high platform, comprised of simple geometric forms and natural materials, to minimize the construction's impact on the surrounding forest. One of the architects' priorities was to retain the bigger trees in order to preserve the original environment as much as possible.

A gravel path leads to an elevated point that provides access to the house. The entrance is aligned with the granite fireplace in the living room, the porch, and the adjacent forest. This axis underscores the relationship between the interior spaces and

BRININSTOOL & LYNCH

BURKHARDT HOUSE

BRIDGMAN, MICHIGAN, USA. 1996   PHOTOGRAPHY: JAMIE PADGETT, KARANT + ASSOCIATES

the surrounding landscape. The kitchen, which adjoins the entrance at a perpendicular angle, has been created using sections of maple. The living room, on a lower level, features glass expanses used as wall sections.

The bedroom is separated from the living room by Japanese-style translucent screens, which create a sense of privacy when closed and an atmosphere of space and continuity when open, leaving the area free of partitions. The bathroom windows were carefully designed so users can enjoy the light and the views without losing any privacy. The guest area is connected to the rest of the house while remaining a discrete space. As with all Brininstool & Lynch designs, the choice of materials is governed by a desire to maximize stability and comfort as well as by significant considerations such as compatibility with the environment and budget. The true nature of the materials is respected and all imitations are rejected.

☐ As with all buildings designed by Brininstool & Lynch, the materials chosen are compatible with the landscape and ensure maximum comfort for the clients. In this particular project, wood was used as a major construction element to create an easy rapport between the house and the landscape.

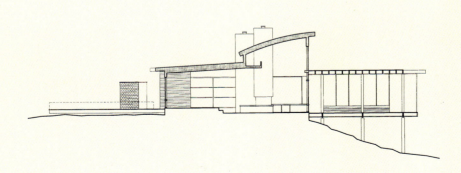

□ Burkhardt House has become part of the landscape thanks to the care with which it was set on the lot. The terraces dominate the site, while the large glass sections create a very close affinity between the interior and the forest.

□ The materials used inside harmonize with those of the main structure and with the tones visible in the surrounding forest.

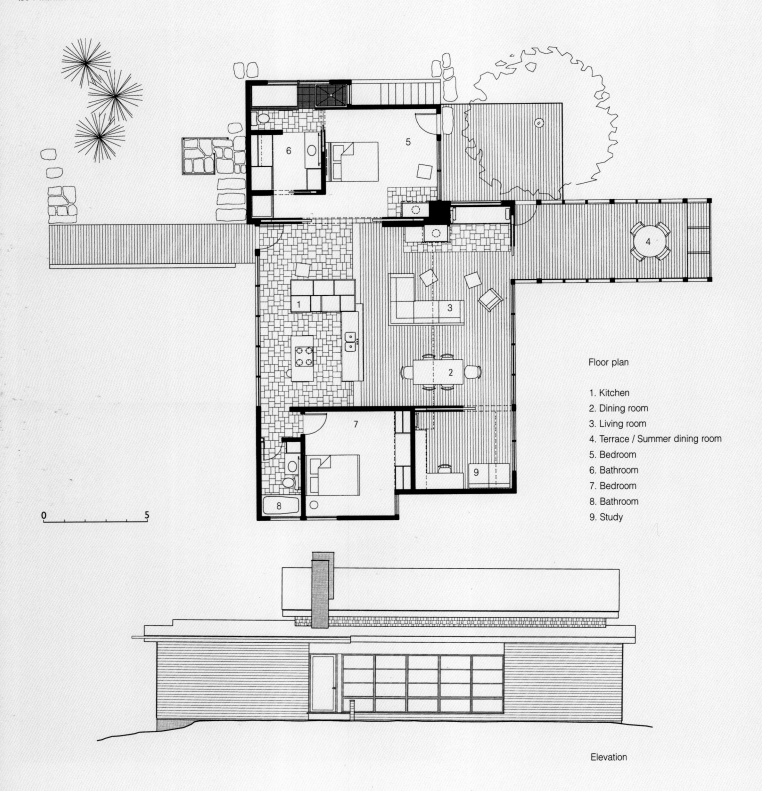

Floor plan

1. Kitchen
2. Dining room
3. Living room
4. Terrace / Summer dining room
5. Bedroom
6. Bathroom
7. Bedroom
8. Bathroom
9. Study

0   5

Elevation

When he commissioned the design for this house, pianist Thomas Larcher specified that it was to be built in an isolated area where there would no danger of his music bothering any neighbors. Consequently, the building was constructed on a site in a remote valley not far from the town of Weerberg, in the middle of the Austrian Tyrol. Since the site is on sloping ground, the lot was relatively inexpensive.

The work plan had to be strictly followed, since the functional requirements were very specific. The client wanted a house with a room large enough for two grand pianos, with appropriate acoustic properties. After lengthy discussions between client and architect, the latter came up with a design in which strong, clear architectural features predominated: the access to the house, the various domestic elements specified by the client, and the interior climatic conditions he desired. As a result of this close cooperation, the project satisfied the needs of the client and allowed the architect to create a conceptual design that was very personal in a formal sense.

Like all other traditional country dwellings in this region, the house is situated on the top of a hill, providing a marvelous view of the magnificent Alpine landscape. The building is set into the ground by means of a system of structural pillars, which minimizes the impact on the immediate surroundings.

The side windows, framed by concrete sections, open up the interior to the bright Alpine light, while the stepped roof covers three spatial divisions in a diagonal arrangement, almost perpendicular to the gradient. A panoramic window in the south wall provides superb views of the beautiful valley. The central area of the house is broken by

MARGARETHE HEUBACHER-SENTOBE

☐ HOUSE FOR A MUSICIAN

WEERBERG, TYROL, AUSTRIA. 1996   PHOTOGRAPHY: MARGHERITA SPILUTTINI

two pillars that define the interior distribution. Between the two thick walls, space is consolidated in particular sectors, each of which forms a peaceful little nook on successive levels. The work area, the heating area with a couch, and the two grand pianos were all placed on the same level as the entrance. The kitchen, dining room, bedroom, and bathroom are located on the floor below. The dining room table and other interior elements are visible from above, due to the two-story space that visually links all the different parts of the house. Since it is the only architectural feature clearly evident to passersby, the flagstone for the balcony employs zinc oxide. All the other materials used in the building are typical of Alpine houses: exposed concrete, natural pine, glass and metallic sheeting for the exterior, white plaster walls, and solid wood floors and ceiling inside. As furniture affects sound within a closed space, to ensure high-quality acoustics, the furnishings were limited to the bare essentials. For the same reason, great care was taken in planning the air conditioning system, and the glass panels were designed to soundproof the house and minimize heat loss.

Even in her early projects, Margarethe Heubacher-Sentobe was fascinated by the effects of the solid bulk of masonry in construction. In her sketches, she emphasizes weight as much as any other architectural element, counterposing it with light, fragile elements. It is precisely these dualities—lightness against heaviness, opacity versus transparency—that create the most interesting details, approaches, and contrasts in her architecture.

□ Access to the house is by a narrow path on the north side of the mountain. The windowless wall on this side is interrupted only by the main door, thus guaranteeing total privacy from people passing along the path.

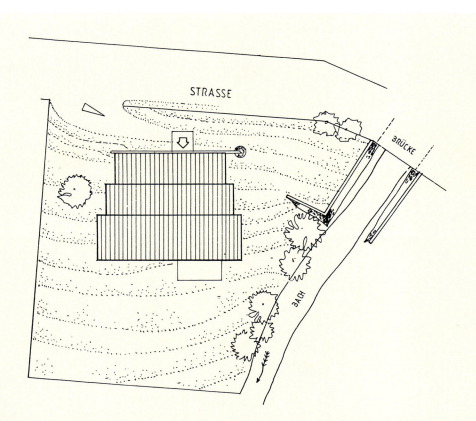

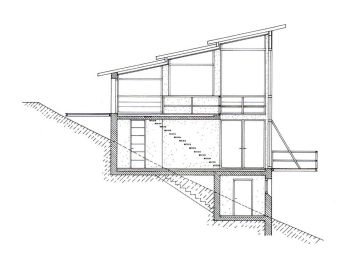

☐ The client insisted on the side walls being almost entirely glass, to make the structure of the house and the interior visible from outside and to provide superb views of the landscape from every interior area.

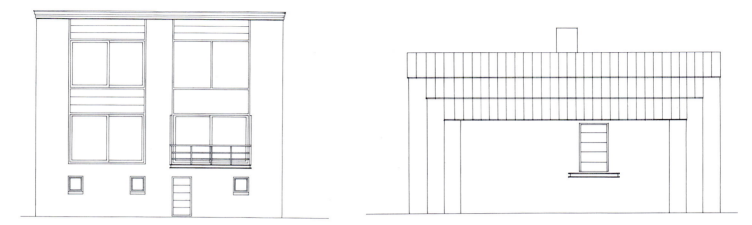

Detail of north and south elevations

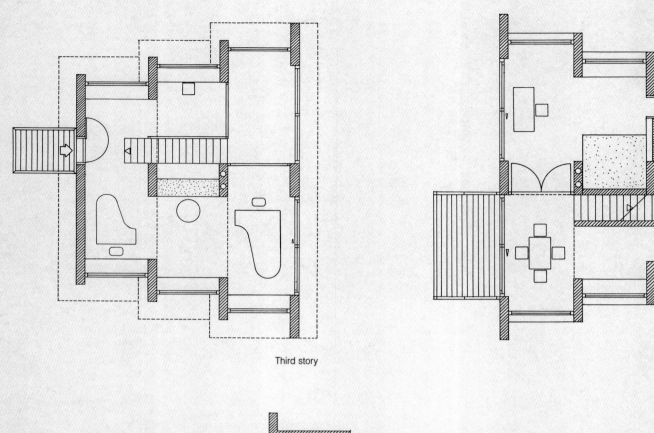

Third story

Second story

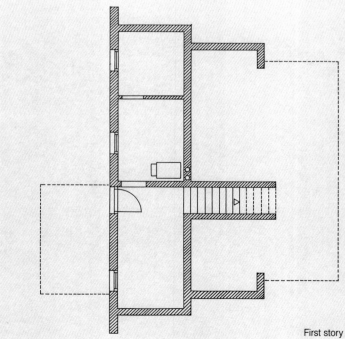

First story

0   5

☐ The magnificent views of the valley filter through the panoramic windows. Since there is so much glass, the design incorporated thermal isolation, which drastically cuts heating costs. Throughout the planning of this project, the architect kept one specific consideration in her mind: the cost-effectiveness of the building process.

☐ Furnishings were limited to a few indispensable pieces, since too many objects in an interior space will affect acoustics, which were of prime importance in this project.

It may not be everybody's idea of Shangri-La, but as an exercise in community living and confronting the so-called "Golden years," the "Cheesecake Consortium" is innovative, challenging, and most admirable. As an architectural exercise, it also presented challenges for the Berkeley firm of Fernau & Hartman, including coping with eleven individuals as "the Client" and working within a rather modest budget. Happily, a great deal of determination and goodwill on both sides led to a smoothly run and successful project that received several awards. One, from the California branch of the American Institute of Architects (AIA)

described it as "a socially innovative, environmentally responsible, and financially viable alternative for community living."

The idea behind the project was to build collective housing so that a group of friends (four couples and three singles) could live together and give each other mutual support in the later years of their lives.

The individuals, currently in their forties, fifties, and sixties, enjoy friendships that go back a long way and that have been thoroughly tested. Most of them still work and live elsewhere but plan to retire here. Set on a 13-acre site in Mendocino County, north of San Francisco, the Cheesecake complex,

built on a flat shelf on the 100-year flood plain of the Navarro River, is surrounded by a redwood forest. The apparently whimsical name actually belongs to the site. The previous owners were an Italian family named Casatas, loosely translated as "cheese pie," and adopted by the local community as "cheesecake."

Architects Richard Fernau and Laura Hartman are known for their imaginative, environmentally friendly projects, collaborative approach, and keen interest in social issues. "We loved the idea of doing housing for a group. This was a project with modest financial parameters, and we wel-

FERNAU & HARTMAN

COLLECTIVE HOUSING FOR THE CHEESECAKE CONSORTIUM

MENDOCINO COUNTY, CALIFORNIA, USA. 1996   PHOTOGRAPHY: RICHARD BARNES, TIM STREET

comed the cost challenges." In turn, they were impressed by the attitude of the group, which was easier to deal with than a single client. Decision making was democratic, but tight and organized.

Though it might seem ironic, the retirement complex has the youthful appearance and spirit of a camp or new settlement, a reflection of the energy behind it. There are communal rooms for sundry activities, and the residents plan to spend time hiking in the forest and playing volleyball. Nevertheless, they are realistic about the future, so the design includes such practical touches as 34-inch-wide doors for wheelchairs, space

for ramps, and an elevator. A shrewd feature is the alternation of public and private areas. For example, to reach the laundry or library, one passes by the individual living quarters, which creates social circulation, and avoids any risk of one member becoming isolated.

There are three main buildings, raised 5 feet off the ground because of the flood plain, a bath house, pool, and tent platform. A garden sits in a separate clearing. The three main buildings are a workshop; a lodge with a communal kitchen, living room, dining room, and office; and a bedroom wing that includes a library and laundry/sewing room.

Interior space exceeds 5,000 square feet and exterior space (verandas, "dog-trot," tent decks, and a pavilion) totals 3,000 square feet. Conscious of the farm building tradition but anxious not to fall into the picturesque, the architects designed a simple, inexpensive structure: a wood frame on concrete pillars, with siding made of painted plywood, cedar-stained battens, and painted corrugated metal. The roof is painted panel and unpainted corrugated metal. When possible, recycled materials were employed. Wood milled from the trees cleared from the site was used for the decking, banisters, and dining table.

☐ There is little likelihood of being neglected by one's family in this attractive, welcoming corner of northern California. It is the antithesis of the conventional retirement home, and the visitors will keep coming.

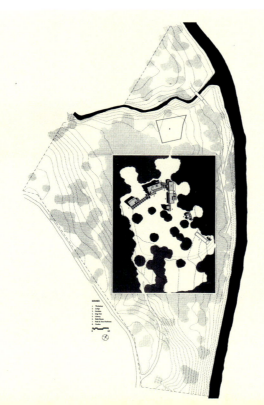

☐ The communal spaces are all subtly designed to cope with influxes of the enormous extended family (26 children and 9 grandchildren at present). Rooms spill out onto wide porches; guests can sleep on the tent platforms or in the "dog-trot" wing (named after the Southern tradition of roofed passages between structures).

Frank Harmon enjoys watching the succession of plants and trees as he drives along the roads winding through Raleigh Forest in Piedmont, North Carolina. These forests, like seasonal barometers, are in a state of perpetual flux. The fast-growing pines shoot up in search of the sunlight blocked by leafy oaks and other large trees.

The houses people build during successive generations evolve in the same way as these forest ecosystems. A house that met the needs of a farmer 50 years ago is not necessarily a residence in which a recently arrived agricultural engineer wants to live. The deciduous forests are gradually disappearing, leaving the space to the emerging vegetation.

Rozelle-Ragan House is a farmhouse that has been turned into a structure that doubles as a suburban residence and work space for the clients. Like many people today, Ron Rozelle and Rosa Ragan work at home. He is a painter; she, a restorer of antiques.

Like the farmers of days gone by who learned carpentry in order to build their dream houses, Ron Rozelle exchanged his palette and paintbrushes for a hammer and nails for three years, during which time he managed to complete almost all of the building work. Architect Frank Harmon wanted the house to recall aspects of the old neighboring farms, but although touches of traditional architecture are visible, the references are not always obvious. The finish of the exterior walls is a modern version of the vertical wood planking of yesteryear. Harmon's version is yellow, in

FRANK HARMON
☐ ROZELLE-RAGAN HOUSE
PIEDMONT, NORTH CAROLINA, USA. 1998   PHOTOGRAPHY: BRYAN HOFFMAN

contrast to the white walls preferred by local farmers. The house was built almost entirely of wood. Some parts of the structure, such as the sliding doors and the corrugated metal sections that comprise the roof, are the same as would be found on any farm building in the region.

However, the interior contains none of these rural references. It resembles an urban artist's loft, blessed with an abundance of light that floods in through the large windows, which also offer stunning forest views. The house has plaster ceilings and interior walls; the floors are oak with a polyurethane finish.

Thanks to the close collaboration between the clients and architect, the number of preparatory sketches the latter needed to draw was halved, and most of the details were thrashed out at meetings the three held on Saturday mornings. The quality of the construction is largely due to the relentless dedication shown by the builder, who became caught up in the work. The doors and window frames are beautifully crafted woodwork. The modest size of the actual living space compared to the area allocated for work space hints at the importance the clients place on their work. It is a flexible, functional space with a balcony that offers magnificent views of the forest. The balcony is a place for rest, where one can watch the birds and listen to the murmurings of the nearby river.

☐ The entire first story of the house is the work area. The clients' studios are located at the far ends of the structure, while they share a central workroom in which they keep their tools.

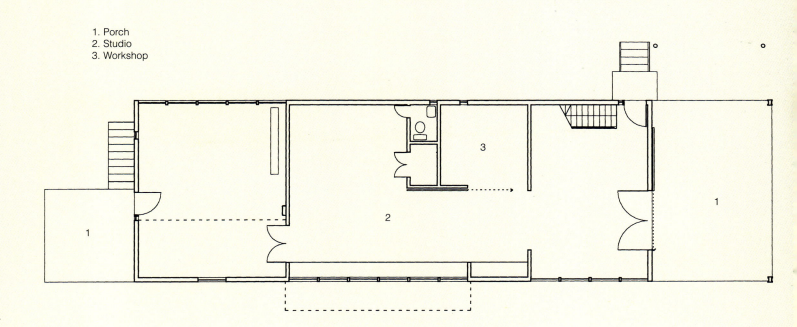

1. Porch
2. Studio
3. Workshop

☐ The antique restoration workshop is near the entrance, convenient when the client needs to use the porch for certain jobs that are better done in the open air, such as paint stripping or any other process involving noxious materials. The porch floor is wood with a fiberglass finish.

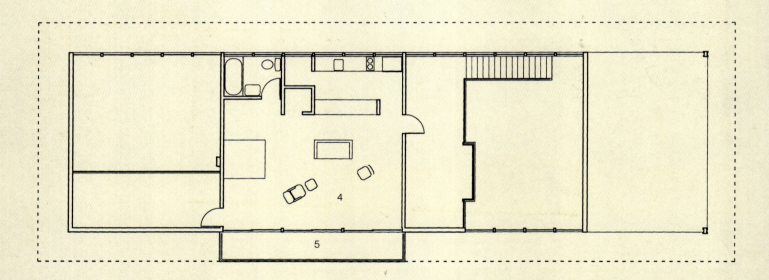

4. Living area
5. Balcony

0   5